The Power of a Woman's Love

The Power of a Woman's Love

Barbara Rice

Fleming H. Revell Company
Old Tappan, New Jersey

Library of Congress Cataloging in Publication Data

Rice, Barbara.
    The power of a woman's love.

    Bibliography: p.
    1. Women—Religious life.   I. Title.
BV4527.R5 1983   248.8′43   82–23061
ISBN 0-8007-1342-7

To my mother, Ethel,
and for my daughter, Rebecca

Contents

Acknowledgments

It takes many people, in addition to the author, to complete a book. With that in mind I wish to thank the women of The Storehouse for first listening and responding enthusiastically to this material, Steve Brown, Bob Terrell, Bruce Larson, Ruth Graham, and Jill Briscoe for their encouragement at pivotal moments in the development of the manuscript, and Wendy Bell for her work with the initial editing. I would also like to thank Dr. Bill Matthews and Dr. Carol Graf for their time and invaluable professional insights as they shared this journey with me. Gail Golding and Mary Hutchins were irreplaceable, typing the manuscript, often late into the night, in order to meet deadlines.

I would also like to thank Tom and Jean Stockton for the use of their summer home during the two weeks I worked most intensively, as well as Lib Adams, Lisa Martin, and Mary Gillam for the days they cared for my children while I wrote.

But most of all I am grateful for my husband, Lucian, and my children, Jonathan and Rebecca, who have loved me, largely without complaint, during the long months I was closeted away with my work. Without their devotion, patience and understanding there would be no book.

Introduction

My friend Barbara Rice writes lucidly and bravely in a wide and winsome way about modern conflicting sexual roles. She wields a creative pen, racing us along the highway of ideas that tumble with originality through the filter of her scriptural insights. She uses rich imagery, likening a woman's inate ability to help, encourage, support, and counsel to that of the Holy Spirit—a lovely touch.

If you read this book—as I hope you will—you may find it points to prejudices you determine are not even there, but you will find as I did that Barbara's disarming honesty sneaks behind the wall of those things we have always believed and helps us discover a garden of flowers we have never before smelled. She forces us to think for ourselves, and that's important—for after all there is a lot at stake—like the challenge of being a woman!

Happy reading,
JILL BRISCOE

Part I

Can Somebody Tell Me Why I'm Here?

"It's a great huge game of chess that's being played—all over the world—if this *is* the world at all, you know. Oh, what fun it is! I wouldn't mind being a Pawn, if only I might join—though of course I should *like* to be a Queen, best."

LEWIS CARROLL
Alice in Wonderland
Through the Looking Glass

1

The Trouble With Being a Woman

The children and I huddled close together against the chill November wind as we watched the majorettes and listened to the high-school band marching past the fire department and the courthouse in the annual day-before-Thanksgiving parade. We were waving to the pretty girls on the First National Bank float and smiling at the homecoming queens who sat on the back of shiny convertibles when I noticed a very ordinary looking two-toned station wagon sandwiched in between the Civitan Club float and the mayor's car. It was being driven by a very embarrassed-looking middle-aged woman, who was keeping her eyes straight ahead; in the backseat her two teenagers' expressions alternated between bashful smiles to the crowd and mortified glares at their mother. When they drove past, I heard a gasp from the woman standing beside me and then a shout, "Mary Lou! What in heaven's name are you doing?" I could hardly wait to hear the answer myself.

Mary Lou rolled down her window and called back, "You'll never believe it. I was bringing the kids home from school, and I made the wrong turn. Now I can't find a way to get out!" We waved her off as she slowly made her way down the parade route.

It reminded me of how I feel, sometimes, about being a woman. It's a difficult time in history to be a woman. We are living through a gray period of twilight and dawn, a transition stage of shadows and winding paths about which there seem to be no maps and few trailblazers who return to tell us the way. With only occasional signposts, like Mary Lou, we find it easy to take the wrong turn. For the first time in history, women face the option of becoming anything we want to be; this has precipitated a crisis, calling for each of us to face difficult questions for which, ultimately, we must all find some answers.

This book results from my search for some answers about my femininity as I grope about in the shadows—sorting out conflicting roles and clashing dreams; trying to discover how to be a godly woman in this newly emerging age; attempting to learn how I should live in it, how I should relate in it, how I should love in it, and how I should work in it. For it is also a very exciting time in history to be a woman.

No one can say women haven't been trying to find some answers. Some of us *have* been rather excessive, but most of us have tried to be cooperative and adaptable as we struggle in the dark. We've read myriads of books, met in small groups and Bible studies, attended retreats and returned home determined to appreciate and admire our husbands and children more. We've even taken the children to the sitter's, soaked in a tub of bubble bath until our skin wrinkled, and wearing filmy negligees, opened front doors to husbands who still have not recovered from the shock. We long to be good mothers, car pooling hundreds of miles each week to take children to enrichment activities ranging from drama classes to tuba lessons. It's a full-time job just keeping up with the suggestions other women have already made.

We sit in the beauty parlor, over our lunch breaks, or in the pediatrician's office, where we dutifully take our children for their regular checkups, and secretly take those magazine quizzes that supposedly tell us if we are keeping the romance in our marriages, are realizing our management skills creatively, or are serving our leftovers attractively. If we fail the tests, we laugh at ourselves for even taking them, but go home determined to do a better job. Frustrated, we go back to school, look for work, open a cute little boutique, or take up belly dancing. Inside we feel restless and angry. Bombarded by discordant opinions about what we should be, it is difficult to remember who we are. No wonder we feel out of place in our world and with ourselves!

Certainly some very significant pressures complicate the situation. Leafing through those same magazines unearths articles about fathers who want to take more active roles in the day-to-day care of their children or on stress management for the growing number of women who are now employed full-time. Sixty percent of mothers with children under eighteen currently work outside the home all day, and 50 percent of them are mothers of preschoolers. It is estimated that, by 1990, only one in four mothers will be at home full-time. These changes have created many new problems.

In times past the mothering needs of this rising number of "latch-key" children (who come home from elementary school to an empty house) might have been met by a grandmother who lived down the street. Now chances are good Grandmother lives in another state and has a job of her own.

All these changes naturally put a strain on the nuclear family, which has suddenly become one of the last havens of unconditional love and stability. Since the extended-family network of support has largely broken down and neighborhood and community support systems of a simpler society are disappearing, the family is forced to assume more responsibility for the emotional security of its members. And the family is receiving less help than ever before in meeting those needs. Not surprisingly, many families dissolve under so much pressure.

The divorce rate exceeds 50 percent. One in six children now lives in a one-parent home, and research reveals these children are having some significant symptoms. They cause more discipline problems at school, have more health problems, and suffer from more emotional distress than children who live in two-parent homes. Possibly this results from the facts that many are forced to assume adult responsibility prematurely or become emotionally overburdened by lonely parents who relate to them as confidants instead of providing the nurturing they need.

Yet all psychological and sociological data shows that the nuclear family is the foundation for human relationships, the necessary ingredient in establishing the individuality from which a person will relate to the rest of society. We are going to have to come up with some answers to these problems and come up with them soon.

"If things were only the way they used to be," a loud and wistful chorus sings out. "If women would only get back in the home, where they belong, we'd all be fine," many others add, drawing a battle line between women who work outside the home and those who work in it. To resolve this conflict, the individual, caught between her feelings of responsibility to her family and her need for her own identity in the world, often attempts a giant juggling act in which she is usually the loser. Rather than face the difficult task of finding new patterns, she merely adds new jobs to her old ones, until, exhausted, she totally collapses.

Left in the morning by the rest of the family, who go out into the "real" world of work and school, a homemaker feels cut off and abandoned, filling the hours it no longer takes her to complete her housework with too many activities or with watching soap-opera characters through whom she lives vicariously. If she watches the commercials, she sees the typical housewife portrayed as an imbecile who always chooses the wrong product, embarrasses her family with rings around the collars, or serves a meal on dull china. Her glasses have spots on them, and all she seems to be able to do right is offer her family prepackaged food or the proper toothpaste. No wonder women turn away from these traditional roles.

Those over forty seem especially disoriented, wondering if their lives have been a complete waste.

"I feel as though I got to the middle of a game, and all the rules changed," Ruth lamented. "Now it's too late for me to go back and start over again."

An unusually gifted woman, Ruth largely ignored her many talents, until her children were grown. She was hurt and stunned to hear her eighteen-year-old daughter say, "Mom, I can't believe you wasted so much time staying home with us instead of pursuing your career before now. I'll never do it that way." Ruth might not realize that this same daughter will later agonize with her best friend, "I know I want to have a career. I never want to be trapped for so many years, like Mom. But I also want to get married and have babies. I'm not sure how I'm going to be able to work it all out."

Modern pressures also affect the relationship between the sexes. An alarming number of young men and women voice deep fears regarding an intimate relationship. They fear the boundaries of marriage. They fear making commitments. Impotence and frigidity are becoming increasing problems in spite of the last decade's rash of books on sexual techniques. Many couples have mastered the mechanics of sex; but it appears few have discovered the deeper satisfaction that comes from a total sexual response of soul, spirit, and body, found only in the give-and-take of an intimate, vulnerable relationship.

Most alarming, however, is what is happening within the hearts of women, in this shifting period. We seem to be in the same place Alice in Wonderland found herself when she stepped into the rabbit's house and drank from the bottle she found near the looking glass. As soon as she drank she began to grow so large her head came through the roof and her arms and legs stuck out the windows. She had outgrown the house.

Women appear to have outgrown the old molds, too, and it is most upsetting, for we are betwixt and between and have not yet discovered how to reconstruct our lives. We live in a gap between what we think we ought to be doing and what we really want to be doing, with our inner and outer worlds unsynchronized. We feel disoriented and empty, restlessly striving to find new ways to solve the emotional conflicts between our need for close relationships and our need to be ourselves. Sometimes we fall off the edges as we search for the balance between these two worlds.

Before we can tackle the outer pressures, the major hurdle women must face is within ourselves. In losing our way we have also lost our self-esteem; we are paralyzed, unable to make the most of our lives or to enable those we love to become their best selves. Our greatest problem of all concerns how we view ourselves as women.

The majority of American women don't seem to like themselves very much. It doesn't matter whether they are homemakers, highly paid executives, or celebrities. The feelings that they should be doing something different, something more, or something better plague them. Although the women's movement has had quite an impact over the past two decades, the average woman seems to have emerged from the skirmishes more insecure and less fulfilled than ever before. Problems with self-image and low self-esteem, with their related problems of depression and alcoholism, are epidemic among women today. Some of these women grab my hand after I speak at conferences, furtively whispering deep longings and fears, and if they are also religious, they express guilt at not being the women they know God wants them to be. The problems produced by low self-esteem affect women in every area of their lives.

These problems distort a woman's feelings about her body. A woman who doesn't like herself will look at her body much as she would at the reflection in the mirror at the amusement park. She firmly believes she is disproportionate—too tall or too small, too fat or too thin, too big breasted or too flat chested—she cannot appreciate her uniqueness. Buying the idea the advertisers sell that to be beautiful she must mimic "the look," she doesn't see that even the models in those glossy pictures can't attain this perfection. Each photograph is painstakingly airbrushed to disguise their natural blemishes. If beautiful also means being under twenty-five and thin, and a woman is over thirty and plump, she will never again completely enjoy a good meal, because she will hate to add the calories. A woman with low self-esteem is forever doomed to think she is ugly.

Such a woman feels intellectually inferior as well and will have a difficult time making her own decision or value judgment. She fears making a mistake and is not prepared to take the responsibility for that. "What would *you* do?" she questions a friend about a moral problem. "Should I marry Tom?" she agonizes with her mother, not trusting her ability to make her own decision.

A poor self-image also affects her spirit. Jesus gave us a simple formula for a successful life: "You shall love the Lord your God with all your heart, and with all your soul, and with all your mind. This is the great and first commandment. And a second is like it, You shall love your neighbor as yourself" (Matthew 22:37–39). When a woman feels she is unacceptable, it is not possible for her to love God with all her heart, soul, and mind, or to properly love her neighbor, because she is unable to love herself.

Janice suffers from the side effects of a poor self-image. A lovely and talented mother of two and the wife of an attorney, she has never believed she was very worthwhile. You detect this as soon as you meet her. Her body language speaks louder than her charming and very correct words. Shoulders slightly bent, her eyes rarely meet yours more than fleetingly, and her words are interspersed with nervous little laughs. She prefaces many of her thoughts with "I'm sorry." She seems sorry to be taking your time and keeping you from someone else.

Janice dresses beautifully however. Clothes are especially important to her, to the point that she buys them compulsively, putting a strain on the family budget and thus on her marriage. She also insists on dressing her children, whom she sees as extensions of herself, with the same care. She attends a Bible study and is active in her church, but she feels uncertain about how God views her.

What causes a Janice? She was the only child of a father who could not keep a job and an ambitious mother. Her mother never meant to push her; she merely wanted for Janice all she felt was missing in her own life. She wanted her to be perfect so that her life would also be perfect. So her mother constantly pointed out all her daughter's shortcomings, giving Janice suggestions about how she could improve. But somehow Janice got the wrong message. Since it seemed whatever she did was never good enough, Janice got the idea she was unacceptable and that her mother didn't really love her, in spite of all her mother's words to the contrary. From time to time Janice felt confused and angry about this, but mostly she just felt guilty. Since guilt is a painful emotion, Janice pushed her feelings aside, determined to try harder to please her mother. Eventually Janice could not separate her mother's unrealistic expectations from her own goals. Expecting the impossible, she became destined for disappointment, and with each failure Janice felt all the more unacceptable and all the more unloved. Eventually she stopped feeling much at all.

When she began to date, Janice was vulnerable to any man who would hold her. Sometimes men took advantage of this, and she let them because it made her believe she was loved when they held her. But strangely, now that she is married, she is frigid. She loves her husband and cannot understand her unresponsiveness.

Perhaps saddest of all, Janice has a daughter of her own. Of course she wants nothing but the best for her. She must be the most popular, the smartest, and the prettiest, so she will receive all the love and acceptance Janice never felt but that her mother so much wanted her to have. Somehow Janice's daughter gets the message that she is never good enough.

Mirror, mirror on the wall, Janice thinks as she sits at her dressing table, *who's the fairest of them all? Can somebody please tell me why I'm here?*

> Someone has altered the script.
> My lines have been changed.
> The other actors are shifting roles.
> They don't come on when they're expected to,
> and they don't say the lines I've written
> and I'm being upstaged.
> I thought I was writing this play
> with a rather nice role for myself,
> small, but juicy
> and some excellent lines.
> But nobody gives me my cues
> and the scenery has been replaced.
> I don't recognize the new sets.
> This isn't the script I was writing.
> I don't understand this plot at all.
>
> To grow up
> is to find
> the small part you are playing
> in this extraordinary drama
> written by
> somebody else.

MADELENE L'ENGLE
The Weather of the Heart
Act III, Scene ii

2

Role Playing

A woman who doesn't have a sense of identity, who feels inadequate, unloved, and valueless, spends most of her time trying to hide behind the mask of some more confident character she believes is better than herself, mastering and playing a role for as long as she can get away with it. Role playing naturally grows out of a poor self-image, and it usually works—for a while.

Everyone likes to pretend to be someone else, occasionally. Roles allow us to express our inner ambitions and act out our hidden desires. They can be a lot of fun. Adolescents frequently try on roles, and one of my favorite pastimes, when I was a teacher, was watching my students adopt various attitudes and personalities as they learned to know who they were. Each morning, I never knew if I would be greeted by the macho man or the sensitive poet, the vamp or the helpless female. Trying on different emotional hats to find what fits is a necessary part of maturity, but roles are never supposed to be substitutes for life. A mask is not meant to be a permanent fixture.

Many women never develop beyond these adolescent games, however. They do not stop hiding behind masks, because playing a role gives them a feeling of control in the midst of the disorientation that results from having no personal identity. It permits them to read from a script that tells them which lines to speak, how to think, and how to feel. But playing a role is trading real life for imaginary control.

Some ritual, a public person, or a mask is necessary of course. It allows us to smile and say we are fine even if we are dying of cancer or have just run over the neighbor's cat. Most of the time people don't really want to know how we are anyway; they only ask to make polite conversation. The social structure is made up of these

23

small rituals to ease the tension of relationships, making life run smoother, like good shock absorbers under a car going over a bumpy road. We especially surround times of intense emotion with rituals. Births, deaths, and marriages all have accompanying rites that occupy our minds and hands until we can deal with our feelings. Most of us can't bear to face life every moment, so we gratefully accept small ceremonies that help us along our way.

However, if life becomes only a ritual, if a role becomes a substitute for living, the one who plays the role risks losing touch with her essential being and with life itself, and this has happened to a lot of women. We have many ways to hide our feelings of inadequacy. Some women become flamboyant individualists, like Sara. "I'll be so outrageous," she announces with her dress, her speech, or her actions, "you won't take me seriously. I will hide my fears behind a bravado of wit, or style, or even self-effacing humor, and if I'm really good at it, perhaps I can also hide my fears from myself." The rest of us laugh at her jokes and envy her flair, but she leaves behind an aftertaste of loneliness. Inadequacy has a way of bleeding through the brassiest exterior.

Other women fill their hours with countless activities, hoping they can ignore their longings and unfulfilled dreams by drowning them out with other thoughts or plans. They try to slay feelings of inferiority with accolades, which they accumulate like silver charms on a sweet-sixteen bracelet. Nights can be bad for women like this. In those moments of darkness as they slip into bed, they often find the tarnished image of themselves haunts and teases their frantic efforts to prove they are of value. Perhaps they will try to muffle the accusing voice with one more glass of wine or with a sleeping pill.

Some women try to compensate for their feelings of inadequacy by people pleasing. That was a favorite with me. They spend a lifetime searching for the missing answers in the responses of those around them, instead of in themselves. After all, when you can't please yourself, or you don't even know who that self is, maybe at least you can please someone else.

Those who become consumed by their poor self-images live in a dark depression. Ann awakes each morning an hour before the alarm goes off, to fight her inner voices. She sighs as she rises, feeling tired even before the day has begun, irritably hurrying her children out the door, forgetting to give them their sweaters, then turning an angry face toward her husband, who has remembered he has another meeting and won't be home for dinner. She will just as quickly crumble in his arms, clinging to his strength and begging him not to leave her all alone. When he goes to work, Ann will sit staring vacantly out the window at nothing at all, spilling tears of frustration and self-pity, hoping the telephone will ring. A picture of depression in her faded jeans and uncombed hair, today Ann won't wear a pretty dress and high-heeled shoes; she won't be putting lipstick on her lips that rarely wear a smile.

If I'm an authority on anything, I guess it's on the subject of role playing, because that's how I lived my life until my first baby came. Fortunately motherhood has a healthy way of revealing even the most lifelike mask. A child recognizes a role immediately. He knows when his mother is not being real but only playing dolls and will pull or push on her mercilessly until he finds the mother he needs somewhere beneath the role. By then I had begun to see roles really don't work very well anyway. Women are never successful in discovering the value and meaning of their femininity as long as they are able to play roles.

At one point I tried to hide my insecurities behind the role of the beauty queen. It was a glamorous role, but terribly time consuming. The mask required so many hours before the mirror, not to mention the tiring fittings in the wardrobe department. I played a supporting role mostly, and it was nice to know other people thought I was pretty, but I could see the beauty queen would have a limited season. Physical beauty doesn't last forever. Ironically I was twenty-eight years old before I believed I was pretty, and by then it was almost too late to enjoy it.

The role I remember the most nostalgically was the dancing queen. When I was nineteen I made my debut at a seated dinner for several hundred people. It was a grand occasion. There were sculptured ice baskets filled with dozens of yellow roses and buffet tables laden with roasts and lobsters. I wore a fairy-princess gown and had nine handsome escorts, dressed in white ties and black tails, with whom I danced to music played by a fourteen-piece orchestra flown into town just for me. That night I dreamed of how glorious it was going to be dancing my way through the rest of my life, surrounded by champagne and flowers and all that money could buy. It was the closest I ever came to being Cinderella, so I'm glad I have the pictures. I still take them out and look at them occasionally.

Every woman needs a moment in her life when she feels like Cinderella, and it doesn't have to be as elaborate an occasion as my moment. But I discovered the sun still sets on those days, too, and the morning after the ball, I awoke with a headache. The party was over. The orchestra was gone. My dress was back in the closet, the escorts now in blue jeans, and I had returned to my summer job on a switchboard at minimum wage. Life had broken in.

It happened the same way to Cinderella. The clock struck twelve, and she went back to the hearth, sweeping up ashes. But in the fairy tales there is always a trump card. You can depend on the good old prince, waiting in the wings, to make your dreams come true. I still held out for that. A lot of women do. I don't care how intelligent or liberated we claim to be.

When I married my husband, Lucian, following his first year in medical school, I assumed I was realistic about his shortcomings, but I still believed in Prince Charming in my heart. It explains something of what happened in the early months of our marriage. It might even explain something about the rising divorce rate. Many disillusioned women merely trade in princes they think turned out to be frogs so they can go out in search of another prince. But men are only human, after all. It's not very fair to try to make princes out of them.

When Lucian and I returned from our honeymoon to our graduate work, I had classes to attend and hundreds of thank-you notes to write for our wedding gifts; my culinary repertoire contained only four main courses, and I had never mopped a floor. As we sat at dinner one evening during those early weeks of marriage, the pressure finally blew. The tuna casserole had been passable. A lighted candle sat on the card table on which we ate, along with a few flowering weeds I had discovered growing next to the clothes-line pole at University Apartments. I had even baked my first cherry pie, feeling one could scarcely be more wifely than that. Suddenly, Lucian let out a howl and held up a small round object and part of a broken tooth. No one had told me to look for *pitted* when you bought a can of cherries at the grocery store.

I began to cry. Nothing was turning out as I expected. As Lucian gathered me into his arms he said, "Honey, I know how hard you're trying, but do you think you could relax a little? I feel as if I've been living on the *Dick Van Dyke Show* and you're Mary Tyler Moore." He was right. I was so busy playing the role of the good little wife I wasn't being a real woman.

But if the fairy tales deceived me, they definitely never prepared a woman to be single. How many waited like Sleeping Beauty, believing real life could only begin if a handsome prince came along and kissed them awake? Suppose the years went by and he never appeared? Was each to become resigned to life as a spectator and never a participant in a world designed to be lived two by two? How was the single woman to find meaning and expression for her femininity? What about the widowed or divorced? Would they spend the years to come as though they had undergone some terrible amputation of self, left forever a half and never a whole person? What did it mean to be a woman?

Going to college in the sixties was a tumultuous experience. Panty raids one spring became marches on the president's home the next. I knew girls who burned bras, smoked pot, and disregarded rules. Some slept around and declared they were living the good life. There was talk that men and women were really exactly the same, but had merely been socialized into different roles. A lot of us tried our hand at playing masculine roles, dressing like men, talking as we thought men talked, and going after men's jobs. We began to get those jobs, too, and to demand equal pay for them. If being important was being like a man, I thought I would be in pretty good shape. I had competed intellectually with men since grade school. I felt I could do as well as most men in that area at least. Yet something nagged at me; something seemed wrong with women trying to find a masculine place in the world. It reminded me of a game of musical chairs in which one chair was always missing. Even then I suspected I might do better withdrawing from the man's game altogether, to discover those things I could do best because I was a woman.

My goal was Phi Beta Kappa, and it would be the most difficult role of all. I think I secretly hoped as I studied I would find the meaning to life. The day I stood in the college chapel and was inducted into that prestigious organization, I half expected to receive a certificate with all the answers to life on the back so I could tell which ones I had missed and which ones I had answered correctly.

Of course not all the roles I played ended with late-night balls and honors. Some took me to rather treacherous territory. Like the prodigal son, I've spent my share of time in the far country, bringing pain to those who love me, but mostly to myself. That's where I discovered suffering can tear the most elaborate mask to shreds. But no matter what the role, it eventually lets you down, because the scripts just haven't been written for a lot of scenes life brings. There are no rituals for handling mid-life crises or mastectomies, no lines to tell you what to say if you discover your husband loves someone else. At times like these, you're on your own, and a woman whose life has been nothing but a role soon discovers she is playing to an empty house, taking little bows to nothingness. When the curtain closes, she is left alone, without a trace of real identity. For even at its best, role playing is like looking through the lens of a camera; you become so involved in taking a picture of some grand event, you miss experiencing it, and life becomes boxed into a three-by-five glossy piece of paper with no peripheral vision.

When I finally ran out of roles to play, I began to seriously reconsider Jesus Christ. Although I had grown up in the church, was baptized as an infant, confirmed in the fourth grade, and regularly attended Sunday-school, when I was sixteen I had decided not to decide about God. I don't know if I was a true agnostic, but calling myself one seemed terribly avant garde. Finally, in the spring of my senior year in college, one night in despair I prayed, "God, if You're there, please show me."

The very next day as I was crossing the street to go to class a green Volkswagen came careening around the corner, barely missing me. It got my attention. Out stepped a tall and remarkably good-looking man who invited me for coffee. Jim also got my attention, and within five minutes he was telling me God loved me and had a plan for my life, which he had almost snuffed out with his little green car. Remembering my prayer from that night before, it *really* got my attention.

Jim told me no amount of good behavior or intellectual striving could fill the gap between God and His Creation, caused when mankind decided we didn't want to play by the rules. He explained that Jesus died to take the punishment we deserved for our disobedience so we could experience the love and fulfillment God originally planned for us.

"That's why Jesus said, 'I am the way, and the truth, and the life,'" Jim explained. "'No one comes to the Father, but by me.' Jesus is God's way back, and all you have to do in order to have a relationship with Him is to thank Him for what He has done for you, ask Him to forgive you for not wanting to live by the rules, either, and invite Him to come into your life to be your friend."

Jim quoted some verses from the Bible and made a very convincing argument, so I decided to try it. I didn't have anything to lose. I asked the historic Jesus of Nazareth to come into my heart; and although I wasn't sure He would, He did quietly enter my life, bringing a clean slate with Him, on which I could write a new beginning. I was born again, and I knew a peace I had never before known. My friends called me a Jesus freak and were convinced I would soon get over it. I never have, for when Jesus came into my life, He began removing my masks, acquainting me with the woman He created me to be.

3

Women and Power

Thousands of women today are trying to solve their problems by simply running away. Abandoning a three-bedroom house in the suburbs, a part-time job, a baffled husband, and distraught children, they run from a structure that no longer fits and from roles they are tired of playing. Some leave with another man, but most get on that bus or pack their clothes in the back of their station wagon alone, trading security for a one-bedroom efficiency apartment furnished with a plastic couch, chipped dishes, and a lonely double bed. They may work as cocktail waitresses at night so they can go back to school during the day.

A woman has to be in a lot of pain to do this, especially when she leaves her children. Even as she goes, she knows an abandoned son may never trust a woman again, and a daughter will be prematurely robbed of her youthfulness, taking over Mom's responsibilities and being placed in the emotionally volatile position of substitute wife for her deserted father. That woman knows her daughter may never forgive this betrayal, and at best it will be years before she can begin to understand the kinds of pressures that can make a mother run.

For every one who actually leaves, there are thousands more who never leave, but who are running away in their heads, searching for the missing pieces of their lives. Many of these women reach for power as a solution to their problems, believing if they had more of their share of the world's power, they would be happier. But when they get it, they find themselves in a different bind.

Growing up in a family of bright and capable women, I had a lot of opportunities to watch women juggling homes with a multitude of outside activities. One of my grandmothers taught classes and lectured around the country. My other grandmother was a writer. My mother is a politician. Two of my aunts have combined families and careers. In addition these women have also headed fund drives and charity bazaars for many worthy causes, all the while attending baseball games and piano recitals and trying to provide support to busy professional husbands. I learned by watching that women have a great deal to offer outside the home as well as in it, and I saw at an early age that those who are given special talents and opportunities have a responsibility to use them. But I have also seen the price these women have had to pay to be Superwomen.

On the other hand I also remember how I felt during the days my children were toddlers. We waited a long time for our babies, and when they came, I was thrilled to be with them. Yet as I spent their nap times picking up toys or rolling the toilet paper back on the roll I couldn't help wondering why I had gone to all the trouble to get a master's degree. I had never even framed the diploma, and if I had, I wouldn't have known where to hang it: in the kitchen, matted with matching wallpaper? I had already put my Phi Beta Kappa key on my charm bracelet. Someone saw it once and asked if it had been my father's. As I spooned strained peaches into Rebecca's mouth and wiped Jonathan's nose I could no longer remember why I had spent all those hours of self-disciplined study in college, missing bridge games in the dorm and late-night trips to the campus grill for lemon pie. That junior honors paper I had been so proud of would hardly make exciting bedtime reading for the children. I felt intellectually shriveled. The most stimulating conversation I had all month had been with the piano tuner, and he wouldn't be back for another year, unless it rained a lot. It's not often you happen into a really meaningful conversation in the grocery store or at the drive-in window of the dry cleaners.

I recall the pride I felt when the census bureau called, shortly after I began to be paid to lecture, to ask me some questions about employment. I had made some money that week. It had been only forty-five dollars, but it had been *my* money, and I spent it on a beautiful blouse I would never have allowed myself to buy otherwise. It didn't occur to me that a good part of my generous husband's salary was also mine, in return for my housekeeping and child-rearing services. I never stopped to consider how much it would cost to replace me. Since society didn't seem to value my role as a homemaker and a mother any longer, I had begun not to value it, either. I heard Christian speakers, who left their families at home to travel across the country and received large honorariums to denounce women who worked. Didn't they have jobs? Weren't they enjoying the money they made and the trips they took?

In a society measuring value and success by the ability to make money and to wield power, it should not be surprising that women who have had the same education as men would also like to feel their lives are a success, that they should want to wield something more powerful than a vacuum cleaner, or that they should want to make their own money.

Many women reach for power for much more vital reasons than intellectual stagnation, however. They don't want to end up like Joan, who sat crying on the loveseat in my living room one Sunday afternoon. She married right out of high school, without any job training. The first year of her marriage, little Johnny came along, followed shortly by Susie and then Billie. Joan enjoyed staying at home with them. She never thought much about it. That was what women were supposed to do. When the children started school, Joan had very capably done some volunteer work. The PTA fund raiser she chaired was the most successful the elementary school had ever had. That made her feel so good about herself.

Joan was completely unprepared when her husband John came home and announced he was leaving her, after nineteen years of marriage, for a woman he had met at the office. He also told her that since he would be sending three children to college, she shouldn't expect much alimony. He suggested she get a job.

What does a woman do when she finds herself in this situation and she has not had a paying job since she baby-sat in high school? "What am I going to do?" Joan cried out helplessly. "How can I compete with younger women who have learned the value of developing marketable skills in addition to being wives and mothers? How will I start again? I always believed John would take care of me."

Twenty-five million women live alone, like Joan. Many will be forced to go on welfare in order to put food on their tables. The issue of whether or not women should work is a lot more complicated than it seems. Is it wrong for women to want to use their minds? Is it wrong for us to want to feel more valued and useful? Is it wrong for us to leave the house to go out into the "real" world, like the rest of the family? Is it wrong for us to want to be prepared to take care of ourselves in case we end up like Joan?

But even when we give ourselves permission, a woman often fails to own her competence. In order to do so, she will have to overcome an ingrained belief that any woman who has a successful career must have done something destructive either to her femininity or to her family, if she has one, in order to get herself there. Margaret Mead adds to this, "If she is beautiful, it is worse. And if she is also feminine there is very little she can be forgiven." It takes a great deal of ego strength to withstand the pressure working against a woman's display of excellence.

I remembered this last summer as I sat by the pool, watching my children dive for pennies. Jane arrived, carrying a sketch pad. She had been taking an art course at the university, and when she hoped no one was watching, she brought it out and began to draw, moving her chair slightly behind the others. A mother chasing her toddler discovered her. Everyone wanted to see what Jane was doing. Silence fell as we looked at her picture, because it revealed talent. Not a small talent, but a rather big one.

"Oh, it's just a little hobby, really," Jane hurriedly said. "Just something I do to keep my hands busy." She obviously felt uncomfortable with our discovery. Jane knew we would never again see her in quite the same way.

To publicly declare herself competent in any field, a woman must not only overcome her fear of success, but also a lifetime of mastering the woman's game. The rules of the game are simple: Be good, but not too good; be pretty, but not too pretty; be smart, but not too smart, or you will be excluded from the herd. If you can learn to play this game well, you might be able to walk that fine line between self-expression and crowd acceptance. Jane had just crossed that line.

Yet just as a woman stops playing that game and steps out to become competent, she risks falling into another dangerous place that can undermine her femininity as much as role playing or a low self-esteem. If she becomes obsessed with her drive for excellence on her road to the top, to the detriment of the meaningful relationships in her life, she also alienates herself from her femininity.

Barbara related her observations of some women she had seen in a large national organization in which she has been a leader. She described many of the women at the top as chic and aggressive, carefully dressed for success and running their lives and their organizations much like a business. Most seemed more focused upon their programs than on the people in those programs; few were good listeners or appeared to be warm, sensitive, or capable of establishing strong relationships in an outwardly observable way. Most didn't seem very feminine. Often there were hostile power plays between these women, much as Betty Friedan describes among the leaders in the women's movement. Quoting one of her co-workers, in her book *The Second Stage,* "You can't count on any woman, once she gets some power, not to sell other women out."

In Greek mythology there are a group of women called the Amazons. These women abandoned marriage and motherhood for a life of living and hunting in the forests. According to the myths, they were so obsessed by their desire for excellence in the hunt that they cut off one breast so the strings of their bows would release more smoothly and accurately. In other words, they removed part of their femininity in the pursuit of their goals.

When a woman begins to value competence above compassion, productivity at the expense of personableness, or achievement above relationships, distrusting colleagues, taking advantage of them, or manipulating them, then excusing her behavior with such statements as, "That's just competition," the pendulum has swung too far in the opposite direction. She discovers the same feelings of dissatisfaction with her life and the same disorientation about her femininity that she felt when she didn't have such power.

How then *does* a woman reconcile her desires for close relationships as wife, mother, or friend and her need to express herself in the world at large?

Anne Morrow Lindbergh wrote in her journal, over forty years ago:

> The problem of the woman and her "work" is still so un-solved. It eats at me perpetually. Soeur Lisi is a perfect person for my children, gives them all they should have. And I have the time to write (in the mornings). But it still is not right be-cause I *should* be giving them what she does (and getting from them what she does!) There cannot be two women important to a child. Either you *are* that woman or you are *not*. . . . I should like to be a full-time Mother and a full-time Artist and a full-time Wife-Companion and also a "Charming Woman" on the side! And to be aware and record it all. I cannot do it all. Some-thing must go—several things probably.

Women still grapple with this question. Our lack of answers wreaks havoc between the sexes, in the lives of millions of chldren, and within the heart of woman herself.

Vicki and I discussed this on an airplane one afternoon as I re-turned from a speaking trip. I noticed her the moment she started down the concourse to the gate. She wore a stunning, lavender three-piece suit, accented to perfection with gold jewelry. Every-thing about her seemed flawless: her hair, her makeup, the tilt of her head. Each woman she passed watched intently as she moved with confidence and grace toward the gate, to board the airplane. In her right hand she carried a soft leather briefcase that perfectly matched the tailored pumps which clicked in measured rhythm as she walked. All about her other women fidgeted nervously, adjust-ing handbags and smoothing invisible wrinkles from their skirts. Was she an attorney, a business executive, a physician on her way to a medical meeting? We all wondered. I soon found out, because her seat on the airplane was next to mine, and she was in the mood to talk.

Vicki was on her way home, for the weekend, from her job as an executive in a large company at the state capital. Her second husband and his sixteen-year-old son lived there, as opposed to Vicki's apartment at the capital, in which she lived Mondays through Fridays. She called herself a commuter wife and explained she had received a substantial promotion, earlier that year, which required her to move. Her husband was firmly entrenched in his own job, they liked their house and friends, and his son was happy in his school. At the same time he had not wanted to stand in the way of his new wife's career. They decided she should move alone, coming home on the weekends, and that they would try this arrangement for one year to see how it worked.

"And how are you managing?" I asked.

Her face became a study in many conflicting emotions as she sighed deeply and replied, "I haven't told Jerry yet, but I'm turning in my resignation at the end of the month. I love my job. It's exactly what I always wanted to do. It makes me feel important, and I enjoy the prestige of my position. But I also love Jerry, and after all the pain I went through with my divorce, making this second marriage work is really important to me. Things went along all right at first, but I can feel the distance beginning to grow between us. Even though we talk on the phone every night, it's just not the same as being together. I wish I didn't have to choose. But I don't think our relationship can survive this over a long period of time. I hope the company will give me back my old job."

Vicki's situation brought up an important question. After we, as women, have learned we can do a competent job in the world, after we have learned how to write our resumes, how to plan a budget, how to manage, and how to sit on a community board, after we have attained our chairmanships and received our promotions, then what? How are we to live? Is there a feminine way of going about life, regardless of our role? Do women have some unique and important characteristics that God has given us by virtue of our sex—characteristics we can use, whether we are presiding at a board meeting or baking cookies with our children? Is there a role model for how to be a woman in the midst of whatever we are doing?

The Lady's in Her Prime

The lady's in her prime.

She doesn't have the time
To watch the trains go by.
She wants to fly,
Fulfilling dreams
That so long lay
Beside old theater tickets,
Faded letters,
And that white bouquet
She threw into the crowd
The day she gave her maidenhood away.

The lady's in her prime.

Without delay
She wants to start her journey
To the sun,
Make up for all the hours of fun
She feels have somehow disappeared
Amid the talcum powder
And the dust
Or dressing on the run
To see a picture show.
Life seems to move too slow
Now that she sees
It is her hour to shine.

The lady's in her prime.

4

God's Role Model: The Holy Spirit

I once heard a story of a young woman and an older gentleman who arrived at the door of a department store at the same time. As the man hurried to open the door the woman was heard to say, "Thanks just the same, but I can open it myself." Stepping aside and smiling at her, with a twinkle in his eye, the gentleman replied, "I'm quite sure that you can, my dear. But it isn't necessary." What *is* necessary in being a woman?

Many of the problems we face in these times result from an overemphasis, by both sexes, of what we consider traditionally masculine aggressive traits. Since the beginning of the Renaissance, mankind has valued the intellectual above the personal, has prized scientific exploration and discovery above friendship, and has emphasized reason to the exclusion of emotion. In the process we have produced a world with a standard of living that those even in the last century would not have dreamed possible. We are close to eradicating disease; we invented machines that enable us to have more time for leisure; we uncovered the mystery of the atom and reached far out into the cosmos. But we also sorely neglected our relationships, and the quality of our lives has become seriously diminished. We produced an often sterile and impersonal world that is too frequently devoid of love. We have overvalued the rights of the individual to the extent that we have forgotten how to live creatively with one another. Now we find that the most critical problems we face in the last quarter of this century can no longer be solved with new technology or brilliant scientific breakthroughs, for they are problems in our relationships with one another. We're going to have to redirect our attention once more to learning how to live together, if we are going to survive.

That's why it is so important we rediscover the value of the feminine dimension of life again, because this dimension forms the relationship side of living: caring for life, nurturing it, protecting it, in contrast to the masculine thrust toward goals. It's the feminine element that is so sorely missing and so desperately needed in our world today.

In Genesis 1:26–28 we read that as God created the first man and woman He said:

"Let us make man in our image, after our likeness; and let them have dominion over the fish of the sea, and over the birds of the air, and over the cattle, and over all the earth, and over every creeping thing that creeps upon the earth." So God created man in his own image, in the image of God he created him; male and female he created them. And God blessed them, and God said to them, "Be fruitful and multiply, and fill the earth and subdue it; and have dominion over the fish of the sea and over the birds of the air and over every living thing that moves upon the earth."

In the beginning God created both the male and the female equally in His image. He commanded both of us to be fruitful, to multiply, and to subdue the earth, and to both of us He gave the authority to rule over all that is in the earth. He stamped each of us with His likeness, as a potter might stamp a clay pot with his signature. He created us to be one with each other, even as He Himself was One. God created the woman because it wasn't good for the man to be alone. He needed a woman to work beside him, complementing and completing him as we all tried to build a world. We were to work together much as the Trinity itself functioned—the Three Persons of the Godhead complementing and completing one another, with love as the great bond between them.

But although the first woman was created from the man and created to be one with him, she was not created a man. The creation story is one of differentiation as well.

Then the Lord God said, "It is not good that the man should be alone; I will make him a helper fit for him." So out of the ground the Lord God formed every beast of the field and every bird of the air, and brought them to the man to see what he would call them; and whatever the man called every living creature, that was its name. The man gave names to all cattle, and to the birds of the air, and to every beast of the field; but for the man there was not found a helper fit for him. So the Lord God caused a deep sleep to fall upon the man, and while he slept took one of his ribs and closed up its place with flesh; and the rib which the Lord God had taken from the man he made into a woman and brought her to the man. Then the man said, "This at last is bone of my bones and flesh of my flesh; she shall be called Woman, because she was taken out of Man."

Genesis 2:18–23

The light was separated from the darkness, the land from the sea, and the woman from the man. She was created to be different from him. God had breathed His life into two separate containers, and the differences between the sexes remain part of what makes life so interesting to this day.

These differences are easily observable even among infants. My Jonathan demonstrates more independence, is more competitive and achievement oriented, and is more objective than my daughter, Rebecca. She is more subjective and passive, more intuitive and yielding, more empathetic and emotional, finding her meaning in life mainly through her relationships. A man seems to need activity to find meaning for his life. Men must have challenges to conquer and battles to win, but women need someone to love.

An ancient noblewoman from Abyssinia once wrote:

How can a man know what a woman's life is? A woman's life is quite different from a man's. God has ordered it so. A man is the same from the time of his circumcision to the time of his withering. He is the same before he has sought out a woman for the first time, and afterwards. But the day when a woman enjoys her first love cuts her in two. She becomes another woman on that day. The man is the same after his first love as he was before. The woman is from the day of her first love another. That continues so all through life. The man spends a night by a woman and goes away. His life and body are always the same. The woman conceives. As a mother she is another person than the woman without child. She carries the fruit of the night for nine months in her body. Something grows. Something grows into her life that never again departs from it. She is a mother. She is and remains a mother even though her child dies, though all her children die. For at one time she carried the child under her heart. And it does not go out of her heart ever again. Not even when it is dead. All this the man does not know; he knows nothing. He does not know the difference before love and after love, before motherhood and after motherhood. He can know nothing. Only a woman can know that and speak of that. That is why we won't be told what to do by our husbands. A woman can only do one thing. She can respect herself. She can keep herself decent. She must always be as her nature is. She must always be maiden and always be mother. Before every love she is a maiden, after every love she is a mother.

Searching through the Bible for some illustrations of the image of God, we can easily find role models for how a man should go about living. God's patience, His perseverance, His righteousness, and His justice as He deals with the nation of Israel are all good examples of how a man should work in the world. As the husband of Israel and the bridegroom of the church, God provides a beautiful illustration of how a man should relate to a wife. And of course there is the perfect example of how to be a good father in the relationship between the heavenly Father and His Son, Jesus. These are all marvelous aids, putting a man in touch with his masculinity and with his purpose for having been created. They also affirm that as a man he has been created in God's image. But what examples within the image of God show a woman how to be feminine? What role models guide us at work or as a wife or a mother?

For centuries women have sought ways to identify more intimately with God, trying to compensate for the largely masculine representation of His image. Since He is most often described as a father or a son, and we will never be fathers or sons, it has been difficult to see how we, too, are like Him. The veneration of the Virgin Mary is a product of this need for a feminine role model. From the early days of the church, women have sought a role model for femininity. As a result today some even recommend that the Bible be rewritten, changing all the personal pronouns for God from He to something more impersonal, to illustrate that His image includes both the male and the female. A close study of the Bible reveals, however, that there are already some very significant feminine images of God to be found there, and perhaps the time has come to give them a greater emphasis. I think they can enable women to better understand our value and our roles, and when we do, we will be better able to begin trying to balance the world with our femininity once again.

Many of these feminine images of God are quite beautiful. Genesis 1:2 describes the Spirit of God brooding over the waters, on that first day of creation, in the same way a mother hen would cluck and hover over her eggs in a nest. God at His most creative is birthing and mothering the world into existence in the same way a chicken hatches an egg or a woman births a baby, fussing over the crib those first few hours of life.

Jesus uses a similar image of Himself when He says, "How often I wanted to gather your children [O Jerusalem] the way a hen gathers her chicks under her wings" (*see* Matthew 23:37), and many theologians describe Jesus as the epitome of the balanced personality, with both masculine and feminine traits. He was tender with children, nurturing any new growth He found in anyone; He had a great sensitivity to the needs of others; He taught creatively, but at the same time had an extraordinary reasoning capacity; and He had a firm dedication and determination to fulfill His mission in the world. Both the Holy Spirit and the Son are depicted in feminine as well as masculine images in the Bible.

In Deuteronomy 32 God the Father is described as a mother

eagle who cares for her young, protecting them and making provision for them at great cost, teaching them to fly—not by pushing them from the nest she has built high in the air, but by stirring them up and carrying them on her wings, until they become accustomed to the heights. A woman understands that kind of love.

Moses describes God as a mother who conceived Israel and carried her in her bosom out of Egypt, as a nurse carries a sucking child, and on several occasions the prophet Isaiah portrays God as a mother who comforts and suckles her young. "Can a woman forget her sucking child, that she should have no compassion on the son of her womb? Even these may forget, yet will I not forget you" (Isaiah 49:15). In fact, one of the names of God is *El Shaddai,* which means "the many breasted one," "the God who is sufficient," and "the one who is enough."

These feminine images are quite different from the masculine attributes that describe God. They reveal another dimension of His character, which is soft, gentle, nurturing, and caring. They also correspond beautifully with the descriptions given of the first woman, Eve. In the book of Genesis we read that the first woman was created essentially for two reasons: to be the helper of mankind and to be the mother of the living. As the helper, she was to assist the man in the task of subduing the earth, and as the mother to the living, she was to fulfill her side of the commandment to be fruitful and to multiply. These two functions were reflected in the two names given to her. She was called *woman,* which meant "help-meet" or "helper suitable to the man," and she was also called *Eve,* which meant "mother to the living."

Traditionally the two functions of the first woman have been translated to mean she was created primarily to be a wife and to bear children. These are certainly wonderful and worthy functions. But to see the role of helper and mother exclusively in these terms is much too narrow. Where does this interpretation leave the single woman or the barren woman, the divorced or the widowed? Does this mean they cannot fulfill the purpose for which they were created? Where does this leave a woman's work outside the home? Does this mean if a woman works in the world, she cannot be feminine and use her feminine gifts for humanity?

Such a narrow view of womanhood has, for centuries, caused women to feel like my friend Emmy, who wrote several years ago:

I am getting older, Lord. I'm considered a spinster. Soon I will be an *old* spinster. It's not *my* choice, dear Lord. I have always wished to become a wife and mother. I have so much love to give. To be sure, I have had boyfriends; I've been in love with a number of them; I would have married some of them; but it never came to pass. No one has ever asked me. I've tried to be pleasant, a good conversationalist; I have been what is called "neat in appearance"; I have been a good listener. I have been neither shy nor forward. So—what is wrong with me? I feel so left out, dear Lord. I feel life has bypassed me, and I resent it.

Obviously there must be ways in which a woman like Emmy can be a helper without being a wife, helping every man and every woman as the helper of mankind. And for those who have never carried a child in their bodies, they should be no less women or less mothers to the living. Surely there are ways in which it is possible to be a mother without ever being a biological mother. But how? What is the essence of being a woman?

When I began to look more deeply into the function of the Holy Spirit as a manifestation of God's image, something clicked for me about my femininity, and I discovered a role model for how a woman can be the helper and the mother for which she was created, regardless of whether she is married or single, whether she works or stays at home, or whether she is childless or is like Old Woman in the Shoe.

When I first began to see the comparison between the feminine and the Holy Spirit, I was dazzled by it. I felt as though I had happened upon the source of a spring, hidden deep within the mountains, amid dark thickets and lush green undergrowth. What I found seemed to be the hidden spot from which the heart of my femininity sprang. Here I discovered the very place upon which God's signature had been written on my life. That moment of insight was like exposing my hidden value as a woman to the bril-

liant light of day, and I was awed by it. I wondered if I could possibly have many of the same important characteristics as the Holy
Spirit, merely because I had been created a woman.

Although the word *Spirit* is often used in the feminine gender in
the Bible, that was clearly not enough upon which to build an analogy. It was far more intriguing to see that the Holy Spirit is also
called the Helper, just as the first woman was. Jesus had said of the
Holy Spirit, "I will ask the Father, and he will give you another
Helper, who will stay with you forever. He is the Spirit, who reveals
the truth . . ." (John 14:16, 17 TEV). As a helper, the Spirit brings
His gifts to the church (Acts 2:38) and His fruit of love, joy, peace,
and patience into our lives (Galatians 5:22). The Spirit sets me free
to be myself, for ". . . where the Spirit of the Lord is, there is liberty"
(2 Corinithians 3:17 NAS).

The word John uses in his Gospel and letters when he calls the
Holy Spirit the Helper is unique, found nowhere else in the Bible.
He uses the Greek word *parakletos,* and John's concept of the Holy
Spirit is called the Paraclete by theologians. As I read William Barclay's study book of New Testament words I could trace the many
facets of this jewel of a word, and as I read its meaning I discovered
that *helper* can also be translated as the *counselor* or as *advocate* and
that these seemed to be two ways in which the Holy Spirit specifically helped. Jesus said the Holy Spirit would teach us all things,
counseling us in the way we should live the Christian life (John
14:26). Moreover the Holy Spirit intercedes for us as an advocate
with the Father (Romans 8:27). In addition to being the Helper, the
Paraclete was also described in some very maternal language, for
another way in which John 14:16, 18 (KJV) is translated is "I will
pray the Father, and he shall give you another Comforter, that he
may abide with you for ever. . . . I will not leave you comfortless."
By Spirit we are initially born into the Christian life (John 3:8), and
the Spirit gives life (John 6:63). In a motherly fashion He helps us in
our weakness, causing us to recognize our adoption as God's children, whereby we cry out *Abba,* the Hebrew child's word for *Daddy,*
to our heavenly Father (Romans 8:15–26). Indeed two additional
translations of *parakletos* are "comforter" and "encourager," and

they express the ways in which the Holy Spirit acts as a mother to the living. As a comforter the Spirit nurtures and protects us, hiding our spiritual lives in Christ, yet as an encourager He also propels us out into the world in service to mankind.

But I knew I would have to be careful not to go too far with this comparison. After all, God is One, the Trinity a plurality acting as a unit, and God's image is in actuality beyond sexual distinction, both male and female but neither male nor female. I could see it would be a grave error to divide the Trinity according to sex. Indeed it would lead to an ancient heresy called modalism, which divided the Godhead into God as the Father, the Holy Spirit as the mother, and Christ as their child. When I discovered this heresy, I got a little nervous. I had visions of myself as Joan of Arc, on a fiery pyre in the middle of our driveway, waving good-bye to Lucian and the children. I didn't want to be a heretic, neither did I want to build an entire theology around this comparison between the Holy Spirit and the feminine, but I could see the analogy was a treasure and that I had found a way in which I had been created in God's image and had found a role model for how to be a woman.

As I thought about this comparison and looked around at my neglected housework I saw many ways in which the Holy Spirit was a feminine image. Remembering that the Bible says our bodies are the temples of the Holy Spirit, I could see that in a way we are His dwelling place, and He lives within us as I live in my house. He constantly remodels my spirit, moving the furniture of my priorities around, mending the broken places in my self-esteem, dusting out the corners of sin, and in general throwing back the curtains to let the holy light of God shine in. The Holy Spirit cleans my spirit just as I do my house, making it a fit dwelling place for the Father and the Son. It is as though the Father has chosen the house, the Son has paid the price for it, and the Holy Spirit has come to live in, to take care of it and to keep it clean. I could really identify with this.

I smiled as I also thought of myself as the advocate in our home, translating Lucian's will to the children and then mediating back for them when they have failed to measure up, sometimes reversing the process and interceding on their behalf with their father. And it was also enlightening to note that the function of the Holy Spirit within the Trinity is similar to Paul's descriptions of the role of women. The Holy Spirit has the same substance as the Father and the Son, equal in power and glory with them, equal in importance to them, but adaptive to their desires, sent by them, and operating in conjunction with them.

But perhaps the most exciting revelation of all was to see that God had empowered me to be a helper and a mother to mankind with the same extraordinary power present in the Holy Spirit: love. I saw for the first time the great power in a woman's love and saw that when I loved by being a helper, a counselor, a comforter, or an encourager, in whatever situation I found myself, those who received this love experienced the love of God poured through a uniquely feminine container. They experienced a little bit of the power of Pentecost.

Recognizing this gave me a fresh glimpse of the great value of my femininity. It enabled me to see potential gifts available to me merely by virtue of the fact I was a woman. I looked beyond my roles and into the core of what it meant to be a woman, and I was excited about discovering new ways to use these gifts. I caught a vision of how we women could go about bringing our feminine selves back into the world by being these counselors and encouragers, these helpers and comforters, and I suddenly felt very valuable in God's eyes. That made me feel more valuable in my own eyes as well.

I hope this will only be the beginning of much more study on the comparison of the feminine with the Holy Spirit, because I believe it is an important analogy. Not only has it been important to me, but I have seen how important it has been in the lives of the women with whom I have shared it. Many have responded like Beth, who came up to me following a lecture to ask, "Do you mean God created me to be all the things I already like to do?" Some of the dismay seemed to disappear from her face. There was a look of satisfaction in her eye, which swept away those feelings that accompany a poor self-image. The look said, "Maybe I'm not so bad, after all."

The Middle-Time

Between the exhilaration of Beginning ...
  And the satisfaction of Concluding,
    Is the Middle-Time
      Of Enduring ... Changing ... Trying ...
        Despairing ... Continuing ... Becoming.

Jesus Christ was the man of God's Middle-Time
  Between Creation and ... Accomplishment.
Through Him God said of Creation,
  "Without mistake."
And of Accomplishment,
  "Without doubt."

And we in our Middle-Times
  of Wondering and Waiting,
    Hurrying and Hesitating,
    Regretting and Revising—
We who have begun many things ...
  and seen but few completed—
We who are becoming more ... and less—
Through the evidence of God's Middle-Time
  Have a stabilizing hint
    That we are not mistakes,
    That we are irreplaceable,
    That our Being is of interest,
      and our Doing is of purpose,
    That our Being and our Doing
      are surrounded by Amen.

Jesus Christ is the Completer
  of unfinished people
  with unfinished work
  in unfinished times.

May He keep us from sinking, and from ceasing,
  from wasting, from solidifying,
That we may be for Him
  Experimenters, Enablers, Encouragers,
  and Associates in Accomplishment.

                                        LONA FOWLER

Part II

The Way of All Women

How can women bring warmth back into this cold, impersonal machine-like world? Surely by being more themselves, by exploring the world in their way, by feeling it in their way, by understanding life in their way.

PAUL TOURNIER
The Gift of Feeling

5

Women as Counselors

Perhaps the most obvious way in which a woman has been created as a counterpart and a helper for a man is in her special ability to be a counselor. A wise woman, who comes alongside a man to advise him and who counsels him well, is an invaluable asset to him. God planned for us to do this. One of the reasons God said it wasn't good for the man to be alone was because he needs the feminine point of view for balance. He may not always like it, but he needs it.

Men and women really don't think a lot alike. This hard-to-miss, marvelous, and often frustrating fact of life is one reason we have trouble understanding each other. I see it at my home every time the scientist's point of view butts heads with the poet's. Lucian approaches any problem much more directly and in a more clearcut fashion than the intuitive and evolutionary way I like to look at the world. His thinking tends more toward the scientific and orderly than mine. He finds pleasure packaging his ideas into tidy little compartments, whereas I like to look at the total picture, focusing on the subtleties and the ambiguities, which never bother me a bit. You could say I think in a less definite way.

Elizabeth put her finger on this unique difference one day as she cleaned the grease from around my stove. Her soft brown face was set in that no-nonsense look she has when she does what she calls the heavy cleaning for me, every other Monday. I asked her to tell me how she felt about being a woman.

"Miz Rice, being a woman is the most wonderful thing in the world."

"Why do you think so, Elizabeth?" I asked.

"Because women just knows things men don't know, that's all," she answered with all her common-sense wisdom.

Actually the feminine dimension within both sexes is the vision-ary. Intuition prompted Jesus to ask, "Who touched me?" of the woman with the issue of blood, although He was being pressed on all sides by a large crowd. It was this "knowing without knowing how it knows" that enabled Joseph to interpret dreams and John to receive the revelation at Patmos. But often it is a woman who first looks inward to find meaning in any given situation, and this en-ables her to interpret mysteries for others, putting them in touch with their own inner worlds. It is one of the most beautiful functions of womanhood.

Of course we all share the capacity to think in both ways. We all contain the potential to be both reasonable and creative. But one of the problems women currently face is that most of us have had a lot more practice in the masculine way of thinking, because our schools have taught it for so many years. This stifles our creativity and causes many of us to be so rational we forget how to use our intui-tion. It especially cuts off women from our ability to think in our own feminine way and keeps us from being able to properly mirror and counsel mankind from our feminine point of view. Society has thus lost much of the variety and color that comes only by combin-ing the masculine with the feminine. For where reason reigns un-checked, we find the mechanical and sterile world we have pro-duced today. Tragically, so many of us have lost our ability to use, value, and trust this God-given feminine wisdom.

Reason has not always been valued above intuition, however. Many cultures greatly prize the wisdom that comes from "knowing without knowing how it knows," which is the hallmark of feminine thinking. It is often called instinct or common sense and comes from an ability to listen to the heart and to hear words from the heart of another. Women have traditionally excelled in this capac-ity, to the degree it is sometimes called woman's intuition. Pediatri-cians have learned to respect this sort of thinking, knowing that sometimes mothers just know about their children things for which there is no rational explanation.

There exist many biblical examples of a woman's intuitive knowledge. Mary journeyed alone through the hill country, to her cousin Elizabeth, to receive the confirmation that she carried the

Messiah in her body. Jesus first revealed His divinity to the woman at the well. Mary was the first to understand there would be a Calvary and anointed Christ for burial with her most expensive perfume. It was to the women the angel appeared at the tomb, announcing the good news of the risen Christ. But when these women joyfully ran to the disciples, to tell them the news, the disciples had to wait for scientific evidence before they would believe. Thomas even had to touch the hands of Christ.

This instinct is probably closely related to whatever causes a bird to return to the same nest each year or tells a caterpillar when to cocoon and how to make that cocoon. That inner push from within causes us to become and to be what we were created to be. Animals operate almost exclusively from instinct, but we humans have it, too, and women seem to have been given an extra measure of instinct to enable us to fulfill our God-given role as counselors.

Although all creation was created primarily to glorify God, unlike anything else in creation, women were given an additional job description. We were also created to glorify man. First Corinthians 11:7, 8 (NAS) says, "A man ought not to have his head covered, since he is the image and glory of God; but the woman is the glory of man. For man does not originate from woman, but woman from man; for indeed man was not created for the woman's sake, but woman for the man's sake." In addition to glorifying God, the woman is to be the halo of man as she mirrors or reflects all she sees in him, his failures and his godliness, so he can see himself more clearly and grow into the man God created him to be.

It is easy to see how useful this kind of wisdom can be in a marriage relationship! But every committee ought to have at least one woman on it for all of these same reasons, too. When Lucian gives me the opportunity, I can tell him quite a lot about the character of those with whom he associates. Women pick up the intentions of someone's heart much more quickly than men can. When my wisdom is not being colored by prejudices and jealousies, I can give Lucian a clearer vision of his facts, when he is trying to make a decision, because I am not as disturbed by contradictions as he is. But perhaps most importantly I can help him understand feelings and find the right words to express his own feelings. Men today desperately need to be more in touch with their feelings.

Women continually complain to me about cold and aloof husbands. But often we fail to recognize that our husbands seem unfeeling, not because they want to be, but because they don't know how to get in touch with their emotions. Sometimes they simply don't know how they feel until they have been confronted by our emotions and have responded to them. Women find this hard to believe, but it's true.

Sometimes women find counseling difficult, however, because we often have trouble expressing our deepest truths. These truths are sometimes accompanied by tears, with which men are not always comfortable. Susie once told me, "I have learned never, never to cry in front of my husband. It completely unglues him." That is such a shame because chances are good Susie's husband is deprived of one of his wife's greatest gifts, because he fears the emotions that accompany her intuitive wisdom.

Marietta has somehow managed to hang on to her intuition. Maybe that's one reason she has such sensitivity and appreciation for the little things in life. She seems to feel life more intensely than many of us. Enthralled by all the sights and sounds and smells of life, she makes you feel more alive just being with her. That makes it especially hard to deal with the fact she is forty-two and battling cancer.

We talked about her feelings one perfect fall day when the two of us shared a picnic. The air was clear and bright, and though the leaves were already brown, the sun shone warmly on our faces as we leaned against the rough bark of a giant tree. Our shoulders touched un-self-consciously as we ate juicy pears and thick slices of cheese and watched the spiders scurrying across the grass. There was a wistful tone in her voice when she spoke of her husband and children.

"I know if I die Bill will be able to take good care of the children, but I grieve over their loss of those things only a woman can give them. Even the most nurturing man can never be a mother, can never pass along the same kind of wisdom that a woman can. Billy said to me recently, 'You can't die yet, Mom. You're not finished with us yet. Daddy is wonderful, but we need you for balance. There are some things nobody but you can give us, Mom.' "

As my maid, Elizabeth, would say, "Women just knows things that men don't know, that's all."

It is in our capacity as counselors that women become like light bearers, raising the lamp of insight in our homes, at the office, on a committee, in church, in any relationship. And each one of us must choose how we will use this lamp. We can hide our lights under a bushel. We can use our insights glaringly and unlovingly and blind those around us. Or we can become like soft candlelight, casting a warm glow of love on all we meet, lighting up their self-worth, lighting up their self-knowledge, perhaps even lighting a path to the springs where the living water of God lies, waiting to be drunk by all who come in search of meaning for their lives. We can choose to allow the Light of the World to be the spark that lights our lanterns, shedding God's compassion and His understanding upon our darkening world.

It is the responsibility of the older women to teach us younger ones how to be effective counselors, because learning how to adjust our wick of insight only comes from many years of practice and experience. This is part of what I believe Paul meant when he said, "Bid the older women likewise to be reverent in behavior, not slanderers or slaves to drink; they are to teach what is good, and so train the young women to love their husbands and children, to be sensible, chaste, domestic, kind, and submissive to their husbands, that the word of God may not be discredited" (Titus 2:3–5).

I have seen so many older widows who feel useless and lonely, cut off from family members, who live hundreds of miles away. I've watched them taking out the pictures of grandchildren they miss and rarely see. If only they would open their eyes and see the struggle and confusion in the eyes of the young women around them. If only they would see how much we need their counsel. If only more would be like Pat, who has adopted surrogate daughters and granddaughters, taking seriously her responsibility and privilege of teaching the younger women how to love. She knows the value of her hard-earned wisdom, and she makes herself vulnerable enough to share those mistakes she wishes she hadn't made with her own family, helping her young friends to take another road.

God has created women to shed our lights as counselors, and we are needed as never before to stir awareness to the value of feelings, relationships, and intuitive wisdom. We must encourage all mankind to slow down, listening once more to our instincts, so their use can lead to the enhancing of everyone's quality of life.

6

Women as Helpers

No Greater Love
In going or in giving,
In dying or in living,
I'll try to show the world it has a friend.
By praying and by caring,
By reaching out and sharing,
The love of Christ will go on without end, without end.

There is no greater love than this,
No greater love than this,
That a man should give his life to save another.
There is no greater love than this,
No greater love than this,
Make me willing Lord, at least to help my brother.

RALPH CARMICHAEL

Women have not only been created to counsel, we have also been created to give. Life flows through us, and we feel compelled to share it, as a mother with her breast filled with milk is compelled to nurse her child. This need to give suits so beautifully the second way in which a woman can be a helper to mankind: by active service.

Jesus said that whoever would be great among us would be a servant. But many women are afraid to serve today, because they fear *servanthood* and *slavery* are synonymous. This results largely from the way in which, over the centuries, many men have abused a woman's natural quality of adaptability, selfishly taking advantage of this expression of a woman's love. Servanthood and slavery sometimes have been the same, but they don't have to be.

A slave is owned by another, forced to submit to every command, having no choice in the matter of how he will serve. This destructive relationship for both the slave and the owner breeds anger, resentment, and egocentricity. A servant, however, chooses to serve and recognizes his value and the value of his service. He is strong enough to look beyond his own needs to the needs of another. A good servant need not always be in the position of power to know his worth. Filled with an assurance that he is loved, he has an excess of love to share.

A servant is an ally who comes along to assist with a job by being willing to be a partner, pulling together with someone in a complementary way. This requires the ability to adapt and to be able to work cooperatively with someone else, and women are the more adaptable and flexible of the two sexes. We have a capacity, like the soft earth in early spring, to be pliable and receptive to seeds of new growth. This enables us to act as good wives and mothers. Bending our needs around the needs of others, we instinctively know new growth can't sprout with too much rigidness. We are able to find pleasure in deferring to someone else, letting him go first as an expression of our love.

Any woman who has ever been in love knows she wants to serve the man she loves in some tangible way, meeting his needs for a good meal, for a good conversation, or for good sex. She may endure real discomfort on occasion to adapt to his schedule, and she can postpone her own desires as a statement of her love. Being a helper, or servant, is being a vessel of strength. A woman knows her man deeply needs to believe he has an ally and a supporter as he forges ahead in life. By her service she makes him stronger and she becomes stronger herself, because through giving she experiences her own femininity.

For Christians, having this servant attitude comes from God so profoundly meeting our needs we no longer fear that by giving we will lose all we have. Released from childish selfishness and fears, we can serve out of the purest form of self-love, and we discover that we ourselves are helped even as our service pours through us and into the lives of others. In the final analysis, in giving a woman best expresses her love, because in giving she shares herself, whether she is giving birth to another human being, giving expert professional advice, or just giving a kind word. God calls both male and female to service, but women seem especially gifted with the capacity to fill up the cracks, crevices, and the empty spaces in the lives of all around them.

Toni Griffin has learned the secret to being this kind of helper. Quick-witted, strong-minded and openhearted, although she remains single, Toni has been a helpmeet and a mother to hundreds. Her house at the lake is often filled to the brim with all sorts of people. After many years as a career woman, she retired early, bringing those gifts she used so successfully in the business world into a form of full-time Christian service she operates right out of her kitchen. Toni uses her home, her casseroles, and her sailboat to support and strengthen everyone around her. Believing God chooses everyone for a special task, Toni sees her lifework as bringing pleasure to others. The last time I sat talking with her, rocking in a comfortable wooden chair on her back porch as I sipped a second cup of coffee and watched the sunlight dance on the lake, she busily clipped through the newspaper, cutting out jokes to send to shut-in friends. Toni thinks about the fact that husbands and wives seldom have their picture taken together, so she likes to do that, and later sends the couple a copy for a surprise. She regularly invites singles up for weekends of fishing, sailing, skiing, or just rocking, and the working girls get pampered as though they were at the finest hotel. She does the same for mothers of young children. Who else but Toni would hurry you out the door for an afternoon of fun while she feeds and bathes that infant you haven't been away from in several months? Who else insists upon getting up in the middle of the night with your toddler, so you can sleep, and then again at the crack of dawn to give him his cereal while she feeds your baby a bottle so you enjoy the unspeakable pleasure of just lying in bed alone for a few minutes, listening to the birds? Who but Toni would even invite you to come for a weekend with a toddler and an infant? Her eyes always looking for new ways in which she can express her love in a practical creative way, Toni is abundantly gifted with the gift of helps Paul describes. Not only does she identify the needs of others, but just as important, she meets those needs in such a way she never makes anyone feel uncomfortable about it.

Toni serves, and in her serving she both worships and glorifies God. Like Paul, she could say, although she never would, "I am poured out as a sacrificial offering upon the altar of your faith." She becomes as broken bread and spilled-out wine in the lives of all around her, and we are strengthened as we relate to her freely shared love of life. Long ago Toni took seriously Jesus' instructions to love one another as He has loved us, and she grew enough in her own sense of self-worth that she knew how to put away her childish ways and put on God's kind of love. Toni realized that love also meant servanthood. She's the kind of helper every woman could be. Deep down we all know this about ourselves, and we don't need a house at the lake to meet the needs in the lives of the people around us. We can help by beginning in our own home or with the person right next door.

Jesus not only called us to be servants, however; He also called us to be friends and learning how to be a friend is one of the best ways to help mankind. When a man approaches a job, he looks at what needs to be done. But when a woman approaches a task, she looks at the person for whom she is doing the job. For this reason we women need more feedback about the kind of job we're doing and need to feel our work is appreciated. Whether we act as attorneys or housewives, we fulfill our responsibilities for someone instead of for something. We generally approach each task as though we do it for a friend. So it is especially distressing that many women are increasingly losing the ability to be a friend. An unhealthy competitiveness and wariness have developed in its place. In the search for power in the world at large, many women have abandoned the equally important world of relationships. We step on one another, are jealous of one another, and manipulate and compete for power with one another.

Traditionally women have provided elaborate support systems such as the one Toni provides for her friends. A woman's special sensitivity discerns human needs, and her earthy practicality tells her how to go about specifically meeting those needs. Throughout history women have endured largely by helping one another carry the water jars from the well, harvest the crops, store the food, and care for the children. Women have always been there for each other in times of crisis and have helped and counseled one another in times of need. Women are very important to one another. Our feminine spirits still cry out for the kind of love, support, and comfort that can only come from another woman.

The lack of understanding, regarding friendship, by both sexes, however, is surely one of the most tragic by-products of our modern society. Have we all forgotten the nuances and complexities that are possible in a loving relationship? Perhaps part of the problem lies in the fact that neighbors one could count on are no longer there. In a typical neighborhood today, one in five homes will change families each year. Over a five-year period, there can be as much as a 50 percent turnover. When you consider the number of women who now work all day, it becomes apparent we just don't have the time to establish the kind of loving relationships that enable us to be helpers to one another.

But there is a more deep-seated problem as well. Have we all regressed, expressing our love in only one of its forms—eroticism—no longer remembering that the love between friends, such as David and Jonathan, Ruth and Naomi, or Jesus and Mary Magdalene, can be as powerful as the love between lovers or between a parent and a child? Is our society reduced to expressing love only sexually?

Perhaps this is behind the increase in the number of lesbian and homosexual relationships we see today. Perhaps it is also a factor in the alarming rise of incest in our country or the increasing number of Americans involved in extramarital affairs. We seem to have lost our understanding of the value and nature of brotherly love, which was the foundation for relationship between the members of the early church. Confusing the love of friendship with erotic love, all too often we maliciously suspect that two friends are expressing their love sexually, or we fear intimate relationships or touching one another because we forget the great wealth of ways in which we can show love to one another.

Ginny knows how to be a real friend. By being my girl friend, she is teaching me to be a friend also. Although she doesn't always agree with me, she always supports me—not only through my joys, but also through my struggles. She's not intimidated by the thunderstorms in my life, coming around only when the sun shines. Encouraging me, seeing the best in me, and longing for me to become my best, my successes don't threaten her. She is proud of me, and my failures never bother her overly much, either. But she won't let me get away with them. Walking beside me, she never remains indifferent, and that's how I know she loves me. Ginny fulfills all the roles God meant for a woman to fill for another woman.

Women are more knowledgeable about relationships than men, and it is up to us to help society rediscover the great variety of ways in which we may express love. We must take the lead, and we can begin by solving the problems in our relationships with one another. As we begin to feel so good about ourselves that we can reach out to one another once again, encouraging, comforting, and counseling each other, we will see a lot more women like Ginny.

Not only are women good servants and good friends, however, there is also a third way in which every woman can be the helper to mankind: by being a good advocate. Women have acted in this capacity throughout history, spearheading many great humanitarian movements. Believing in someone, speaking on his behalf, and pleading his case, an advocate instructs someone in authority about needs and convinces him of the importance of meeting those needs. It seems God has given each woman a special radar that recognizes human necessities, seeks out the underdog, and longs to help the powerless.

This quality led Esther to risk her life by coming uninvited before King Xerxes, to plead for the safety of the Jews. In so doing, she saved an entire nation. By being an advocate, Florence Nightingale saw the needs of the sick and the dying and began the nursing profession. Because she noticed the tired, pinched faces of children who worked day and night in sweat shops, a rich man's daughter, Jane Addams, founded Hull House and then worked to change the child-labor laws. And one nun, small in stature but mighty in spirit, heard the cries of the starving, the abandoned, and the dying in

India, advocating for these people and becoming Mother Theresa. Women took to the streets during the Vietnam War and the war in Ireland, not so much to take political sides as to cry out, "War is not healthy for children and other living things."

Each woman's instinctive drive to nurture the unprotected motivates her to become a defender and an intercessor. Although many of us will never appear before a court of law or a legislature on behalf of the needy, we are being advocates each time we shut the door to our bedrooms and come before our God with our concerns. It would be difficult to say how many lives Corrie ten Boom saved, in the concentration camp, simply because of her prayers. Countless lives will be saved in eternity because some woman loved that son in prison or that daughter headed in the wrong direction and diligently interceded with God on that child's behalf. The Bible says the prayers of a righteous man availeth much. So do the prayers of a righteous woman, when she serves as the advocate God created her to be.

Women have been created as counterpoints in the melody of mankind. We are the contrasting point of view that, when we blend our voices in harmony, creates a chorale more rich and beautiful than a single melody. In counseling, serving, interceding, and befriending, let us sing our songs so that we enrich, enliven, and complete all around us using our gift as the helpers to mankind, glorifying God and man.

> Tune Thou my harp;
> There is not, Lord, could never be,
> The skill in me.
>
> Tune Thou my harp,
> That it may play Thy melody,
> Thy harmony.
>
> Tune Thou my harp;
> O Spirit, breathe Thy thought through me,
> As pleaseth Thee.

AMY CARMICHAEL

7

Women as Comforters

But what of mothering? How can women be the mothers to the living in our world, as well as the helpers? What does it mean to be that multifaceted creature called a mother? What enables a woman to wait patiently as her child tries on twenty pairs of school shoes, on a hot August day, and turns down the only pair that fits, because he can feel the label on the bottom? What keeps his mother from laughing as she asks the salesman if he has any socks that don't get bumpy when you wash them, because her son won't wear bumpy socks? What enables her to realize, in the midst of all this, the real problem is that school is starting? There won't be any more going barefoot and squeezing little toes in the mud, and this is really a ritual of small griefs and worries her son is going through. A good mother can be a marvelous commodity at times like this.

Ingram's second birthday party reminded me of that recently. His mother planned a swimming party, but shortly after the guests arrived, the plastic wading pool developed a leak. No problem. Mary quickly produced riding toys, bubbles to blow, and a jungle gym to climb. As the children played happily their mothers tried to carry on a conversation. Although interrupted scores of times, they never seemed to miss a beat. One of them sat on a chaise lounge, nursing her infant. That made her two-year-old jealous, so she let her climb up in her lap, too. There seemed to be plenty of room. Another mother automatically knew it was therefore her job to monitor the disputes that periodically erupted between the children, gently reminding them to take turns and share. This enabled Mary to bring out the cupcakes and the Kool-Aid, which of course immediately spilled. But that didn't seem to be a problem, either. She had wisely set up the table outside, and the cloth was made of paper. She would throw it away when she hosed down the driveway, after the party was over.

Watching these women, I remembered how I used to feel when my maid of honor, Mona, would come for her annual visit with her children. Mona had four babies in five years, before I even had a chance to have one. I always stood in awe of her, during the hour after they all arrived at my perfectly appointed, childless home. She would first swoop through the living room, picking up figurines and expensive ashtrays, putting them away. Next she would stick a sack full of Popsicles in my freezer, having stopped at the nearest grocery store on her way to my house to buy them. She knew I would never think about something like Popsicles. Then she would start getting the children busy. One year she produced four giant paint brushes from her suitcase and asked me for a pail. Soon the children were outside, "painting" my house with water. It kept them busy all afternoon and gave us a chance to catch up with each other over a quiet glass of ice tea. Mona's creativity seemed limitless, and she was so efficient about it, too. She told me a mother grew an extra hand with each baby, which atrophied and dropped off only after the child went off to college. After I had my own children, I knew what she meant.

I used to wonder what made a woman want to be a mother and what made her a good mother like Mona. How well I remember mulling over questions like these during the long years of fertility testing I endured when Lucian and I were trying so hard to have children. I thought of them each time I went to another baby shower, and they ran through my mind as I lay in a hospital bed, recovering from surgery we hoped would be successful, but never was. Wondering what it meant to be a mother and why I so desperately wanted to be one seeped into my dreams at night and lay heavily on my heart during the day as the months turned into years and we had no children. Even after we adopted Jonathan and Rebecca and I had finally become a mother, I found I still had questions about my femininity. I still felt out of tune with the rest of nature and with my own womanhood, because I had not carried a child in my body.

I remember the day my friend and doctor, Dave, came into my

room as I lay again in a hospital bed, one month after my thirty-fifth birthday. This time I was having a hysterectomy. He had a little yellow estrogen pill in his hand, and as I saw it I quipped, "So you've come to make me a woman again, have you?" Dave didn't let me get away with that, though. He quickly reminded me a woman was a woman from her heart, and until he removed that, I didn't need to worry. He reminded me you didn't have to have a baby to be a mother, and who should have known that better than the mother of adopted children, anyway? Although Jonathan and Rebecca didn't grow in my body, they had certainly grown in my heart. I am their mother in every way. But even if they never had come into my life, I could still have found ways to be a mother.

Remember Emmy, who agonized over her singleness and felt so left out? She eventually learned how to be a mother to the living without ever having a child. Emmy wrote, "I met Jesus today. He wore a shabby coat. I gave Him one of my three. Jesus came in anguish today, laden with troubles, needing a listening ear and a cheering word. I had intended to go shopping, but I let the shopping wait another day. Jesus got on the bus today, and He looked so tired after a day's hard work. I rose and gave Him my seat. Jesus took me up on the elevator today. He has taken people up and down elevators day in and day out—how many years? I gave Him a cheerful greeting, a deep-felt thank-you, and inquired about His health. I got a letter from Jesus today. He had lost His most loved one. I wrote Him a sympathetic letter this evening, comforting Him and assuring Him of my friendship. And I will keep on writing until I am sure the stinging pain of the first grief has mellowed." Emmy has learned how to look at others in a way that enables her to be a good mother, too.

Basically there seem to be two complementary but different aspects of mothering. On the one hand, a good mother must be able to encourage her young to venture out on their own. This aspect of mother love thrusts out and stimulates. It causes the mother bird to push her fledglings out of the nest, even though they show fear. It invigorates and gives courage, causing her to call out with confidence, "You can do it!" This aspect of motherhood enables a woman to be a good encourager.

On the other hand, a good mother must also be able to shift gears and protect and nurture new growth, carefully keeping it safe, warm, and sheltered. This side of mothering causes the mother lion to fiercely defend her young from harm, until they are old enough to defend themselves. It is tender and compassionate and enables a woman to be a good comforter.

When we think of what it means to be a comforter, we frequently think only of sympathy. But sympathizing is merely part of the job. A comforter should make someone strong again as she consoles, never allowing someone to wallow in self-pity, but inspiring him with hope to go on. Restoring him and lightening his load, she provides whatever he needs, until he is able to provide it for himself. As with counseling and helping, God has given women some special gifts that enable us to be particularly effective in this role. We can immediately think of the many ways in which we comfort our children as we mother them. Nancy is especially good at this. My children love to go to her house. When she talks to them, Nancy has a way of looking them straight in the eye, on their own level, so that they know she takes them seriously. She often touches them lightly as she speaks to them, and that makes them feel accepted. When they ask her a question, she frequently completely stops whatever she is doing and gives them her full attention. The children then feel important. It also doesn't hurt that Nancy has a way of remembering birthdays or of making a point of praising children for any task they have done well, either, however small the job may have been. She mothers by comforting, and she fills up the spaces some of the rest of us leave in their lives.

Lib does the same thing. She has been a surrogate mother to my children during many of the hours I spend away from them, writing about how to be a mother. Lib is a grandmother who loves children. She takes them on special outings, gives them candy, tells them stories, and teaches them values. She's also been mothering me a little bit, too. When I return at the end of a day of work, she gives me fresh tomatoes to take home for supper, hands me articles she thinks might help me with a chapter, or makes me stretch out just for a minute on the chaise lounge on her porch before I go home.

None of us is ever so old we don't appreciate a little comfort. When Lib comforts me, she also restores me and makes me strong again.

Connie and Frances do the same kind of thing, only they seem to specialize in mothering adults who have never been properly mothered as children. Their home has become a resting place for hundreds of women. They call it the Snail's Pace, and many a mother who has felt like a motherless child has been nurtured there. Fed in spirit and in soul, as well as body when they eat Frances's home cooking, they are prayed over, counseled, put to bed at a decent hour, encouraged, and loved. These women go on their way refreshed and ready to do the same for their families once more.

I think when we get to heaven we are going to find a lot of saints who never made the cover of *Time* magazine. Many will be like Connie and Frances or like Lois, who is raising her nine-year-old great-grandchild. When I met Lois at a woman's retreat, I was amazed at the stamina she seemed to have, and as she talked about her grandson, Gary, he was obviously the joy of her life. Having an active nine-year-old boy of my own, I couldn't help asking her how in the world she did it. She quietly answered, "I depend on God every day to give me all I need to be his mother. Of course I had to take him in. I couldn't just let his own mother throw him away, now could I?"

At the same retreat I also met Joyce and as we talked I discovered she and her husband had become surrogate parents for children of missionaries who live overseas. Their home has become the place these children come on weekends and at holidays, when the rest of the students at the boarding school go home. When I asked how Joyce happened to get started with this kind of nurturing, her eyes welled up with tears as she told me how two of her four children had died in tragic accidents. "When they were gone," she said, "it just sort of left an empty space inside me. This is how I have filled it."

But women and children are not the only ones who need comforting. There are ways in which men also need mothering, when it is done in the right way. There are times when a man desperately needs comforting in body, soul, and in spirit—consoling in ways that make him strong again, too. Preparing a good meal for a man is one way a woman can say, "I care." There's something to that old adage about the quickest way to a man's heart being through his stomach. And sex has a comforting quality for a man that perhaps it does not have for a woman. Sex meets his needs for affirmation and closeness that often cannot be met in any other way. Listening to him is another way in which a woman can comfort a man. Nurturing all his intellectual, emotional, or spiritual growth by giving him her undivided attention is a great gift a woman can give a man. Irene d'Castillejo has beautifully stated:

> How precarious men feel and how much the particular man needs his woman to believe in him and to welcome his vision with warmth and tenderness. He looks to her for recognition of his unique personalness, to be trusted, believed in and for his work to be given full value. In so doing she functions in her primary role—helping him to find himself.

A man appreciates finding that his inner thoughts and dreams are being taken seriously by his wife and that she responsively hears and cares about them. I believe many men have stopped communicating because women have stopped really listening.

That everyone needs comfort from someone who loves them unconditionally was well illustrated by the public response to a statue that stands in front of Sam Reeves' office in Fresno, California. The life-sized bronze shows Jesus seated and holding out his arms to three children. The smallest little girl holds a bird in her hand, and a little boy has a slingshot stuck in his back pocket. The sculptor leaves it to our imagination to wonder what happened to the bird. But the way Jesus is seated makes you want to crawl up and sit in his lap, and that is exactly what some have done. One morning Sam arrived at work to find a runaway teenager asleep in Jesus' arms. The policeman who regularly patrols the area reports that vagrants frequently curl up around His feet and lay their heads on His knees. I wanted to climb up there myself, when I first saw this magnificent work of art. We all need comfort at times.

Marjorie Holmes aptly writes:

I'm Tired of Being Strong

Forgive me, Lord, but I'm tired of being some of the things I've tried so hard to be.

I'm tired of being so capable, so efficient. I'm tired of the compliment, "If you want to get something done ask a busy person" (Guess who?).

I'm tired of being considered so patient and understanding that people dump their troubles (and their kids) on me.

I'm tired of being so cheerful. I want to be free to be cross and complain and not get a "buck up, old girl," routine. I'm tired of being my husband's faithful partner and helpmate instead of his playmate.

I'm tired of being considered so independent, so strong.

Sometimes, at least sometimes, Lord, I want to be weak and helpless, able to lean on somebody, able to cry and be comforted.

Lord, I guess there are just times when I want to be a little girl again, running to climb on my mother's lap.

Something very healing takes place when people receive the right kind of comfort. Mothers know the tender care with which we nurse a sick child is just as valuable as an antibiotic, the kiss on the hurt as important as the Band-Aid. Good physicians also know this, and the best ones touch their patients when they make their rounds at the hospital. There is something mysterious about the "laying on of hands" when these hands are used to comfort—perhaps because this kind of comforting can be the essence of one of the finest expressions of love: compassion.

The purest form in which I have ever seen compassion expressed came the day Mr. Blair chose to do his dying. I had gone to the hospital with Lucian, late that Saturday afternoon, because I wanted to tell this wonderful man good-bye. Mr. Blair had slipped into a coma earlier in the day; his breathing was labored; and the end was obviously very near.

What a man he had been. One of the last from an era of noble gentility, he had been a gentleman of the finest sort. Only after his death would his family discover hundreds of people he quietly helped, over the long years of his life. He lived with such dignity, and I wanted him to be able to die the same way. Death can be so undignified.

As I pushed open the door to his room I saw the nurses. There were three of them, and they had come to help him die. The family was also there, but it was the women who seemed to know what to do. One held his hand, another put a cool cloth on his forehead, a third spoke quietly to him, constantly speaking to him, reassuring him she was there and would stay with him. As I watched this scene I felt time slipping away from me. Except for the modern hospital equipment, I might have been watching a scene from any century since the world began. I was watching the comforters doing their job. It made me proud to be a woman.

After Mr. Blair took his last struggled gasp of air and finally rested in the arms of his Creator, one of these women knew just what to say to the family as she gathered them around his bed and led them all in the Lord's Prayer. Now that Mr. Blair was gone, she could no longer comfort him. She would help those he had left behind as they held his hands and said their last good-byes.

Expressing compassion openly by being a good comforter like this doesn't always make us comfortable. But then God never did say if we followed Him and did what He asked that we would be comfortable. I was with a friend once, following her surgery, when she developed complications and her blood pressure suddenly began to drop. It was a terrifying experience for her, because she thought she was dying. As I sensed her panic I heard myself asking, "Do you want me to hold you?" "Oh, please!" came the frantic reply. I tried to put my arms around her as I sat on the edge of her hospital bed, but she wasn't comfortable, and soon my shoulders began to ache painfully. There seemed nothing to do but to slip off my shoes and get into the bed with her. When I did, I could feel her relaxing as she clung to the strength she felt coming from my arms. But already I was wondering how this was going to look when the doctor arrived. I felt a little embarrassed, although I knew my friend needed me, and this was the way she needed me at that moment. When the doctor came hurrying into the room, he did pause as he saw me lying next to his patient. But then he paid me one of the finest compliments I have ever received. As he turned to his patient he said, "I see you've got yourself a friend. A real friend."

In ancient times women often went deep into the forests in search of the healing herbs to bring back to the tribe. It is still the women today who can use love and compassion to heal as the comforters. To do this we must dig down deep enough within ourselves to tap into God's healing love. It is one of the ways in which He has created us to be the mothers to the living.

8

Women as Encouragers

Women are going to make a grave mistake if, in our pushing to find our place in the world, we try to deny the importance of nurturing. It is a tragedy for a woman to come face to face with the biological time clock of motherhood and to realize she has missed her chance to be a mother because she was too busy with her career.

I have seldom heard such pain in a woman's voice as I did when Emily poured out her story to me, one afternoon. She had married at twenty-five, when she was just beginning in a career she loved. By the time she was thirty and ready to start having a family, her marriage was unstable. She knew it would be unwise to get pregnant at that point, and sure enough, two years later she was divorced. Emily continued with her career, and by the time she was thirty-six had achieved all she wanted there. She was thirty-eight before she again met a man she wanted to marry, and Bob was forty-five. He was divorced and had two children who were almost grown. When he and Emily married, they agreed they would have one child, but Emily knew it was only for her sake. Bob had already been a father and was now ready to travel.

They spent the first two years of their marriage getting adjusted to each other. This meant that by the time Emily finally started trying to have a baby, she was forty. After two years with no success, the doctor finally told her was nothing more he could do. It was just too late. But Emily had never meant to go through life without a child. She was heartbroken. Sometimes women just forget how important it is to be mothers, until it's too late.

I thought of this as the sun was about to set over the hazy blue mountains in the distance, the afternoon we visited Will and Susie's farm. They live in the country, with their three children, in a wonderful old house always filled with people. Will practices medicine in the front parlor, and they have a garden and a few animals out back. Will was taking us to see the new lamb, and as he picked it up so the children could feel the soft, brown wool he commented that the mother sheep had been an impossible mother. "She will never hold still long enough to nurse her baby," he said. "We had to tie her up the first week, so the lamb wouldn't starve." She reminded me of some of us who get so busy with our projects and our goals that we don't take the time to mother our children properly. As more and more women go to work there is an ever-increasing danger children will be pushed out on their own too soon, because their mothers won't hold still long enough to be mothers. When we do this, we deprive our children of one of the finest gifts a woman can give: the gift of our encouragement.

Rose McKinney used this gift in a remarkable way. I read about her in the newspaper, and when the story was written she was eighty-four years old. The daughter of a former slave, Rose had an eighth-grade education and had worked hard, all her life, beside her sharecropper husband. She was also the mother of twelve children, and every one of these children had gone to college, one way or another. Rose taught each one to read by the light of a kerosene lamp. They grew up to become teachers, doctors, administrators, and parents. "I always wanted them to be outstanding," Rose said of her children. "I wanted them to be useful men and women. I would pray for them that, when they all got old enough, they would all go to school." One daughter remembers, "I can look back and see my mother always standing at the door. As we left her presence, she said, 'Do your best.' " It is a graphic example of the way in which women can be mothers to the living by being encouragers.

A woman seems to do this almost automatically, whether she is encouraging her children, as Rose did, or merely sitting on the sidelines at the Little League game, yelling out to little Johnny that he can make that hit if he'll just keep his eye on the ball or that he'll do better next time, when he misses the fly in left field. An encourager inspires you and gives you courage. To *en*courage is to *give* courage, and an encourager stirs you up, provokes you to extend your reach, challenges you, and summons forth those gifts you may never have known you had. Encouraging stimulates new growth.

Women have a way of doing this for men as well as children. When the hero in a man is acknowledged, he *feels* like a man, and often it takes a woman's recognition and encouragement for a man to realize he *is* a hero. A woman who uses her power of encouragement well can enable a man to reach for the stars and realize dreams he would not have dared to dream alone. Perhaps this is why so many young girls aspire to be cheerleaders. It's a wonderful outlet for this gift.

Beth and I sat over breakfast, talking about this, the day after she had been cut from the cheerleading squad. I knew just how she felt. I remembered the day I, too, had missed being returned to the cheerleading squad. I thought the world had come to an end, just like Beth. And it wasn't only my pride that had been hurt, either. I really loved to cheer. It made me feel great when my favorite football player made a goal and he knew I was behind him. Although I couldn't make the touchdown myself, when I cheered for Larry and he made a touchdown, it was almost as if we had done it together. I didn't realize, at the time, I was merely being the encourager God had created me to be as a woman.

But I learned an important lesson the year I sat in the bleachers, instead of jumping around down on the field. It was the best season Larry ever had. It didn't take a short skirt and pom-poms for him to know I was behind him, and I learned a woman can sometimes be an encourager just with her presence. Larry became a hero there for a while. And I suspect part of it was because someone believed in his hero potential.

I watched Robbie do the same sort of encouraging for Billie, and it was a beautiful thing to see. When Billie decided he wanted to run for Congress, that wasn't exactly the kind of life Robbie had planned for their two children. But Billie felt he had something to offer—that men like himself had a responsibility to get out and work in government, if they didn't like the way the country was being run. This was something he felt he should do, and when he presented the idea to her, Robbie had a choice. She could have tried to talk him out of running, or she could have halfheartedly agreed to it, but secretly hoped he would lose. Robbie didn't do either one of these things. She knew her attitude would make all the difference in the world to Billie, and as it turned out, it did. So she threw her wholehearted support behind her husband, from the day he signed up to run, until the final returns were in. That often meant long hours of standing in the sun, in high-heeled shoes. It meant eating a lot of dry chicken breasts, up on a platform where everyone could watch her. It meant listening enthusiastically to Billie give the same speech she had heard before and perhaps helped him write. For Robbie it even meant some days riding around the district in a wagon train. But she was a good encourager. She inspired Billie. She gave him courage. And Billie won. She saw the best in Billie, and she helped him to realize it.

As an encourager a woman doesn't really make things grow as much as she enables them to grow by giving the necessary love, support, and space for people to develop in whatever way is unique for them—to develop into God's purposes for their lives. A woman encourages people to become their best, not when she tries to make them conform to her desires for their lives, but when she accommodates herself to the inner law that governs their own particular growth pattern. This isn't always easy. But when a woman does this, she becomes a cocreator with God.

In my kitchen is a cross-stitched plaque with Proverbs 22:6 (KJV) embroidered upon it. "Train up a child in the way he should go: and when he is old, he will not depart from it." The word *train* means "to dedicate" or "to set aside for spiritual purposes." It is the same verb that is used to describe the process Hebrew midwives used to make a newborn infant want to feed. As soon as the child was born, the midwife would rub a mixture of crushed dates and olive oil across the roof of his mouth, and it was believed this stimulated the sucking response. The Hebrews believed it gave the child a desire for life. As mothers one of our main functions should be to create in our children a desire for life, a desire to grow, even a desire to grow away from us.

I think of Elizabeth when I think of being a cocreator with God. I've often wondered what it must have been like to be the mother of John the Baptist. I'm sure it was hard on her. Elizabeth probably thought it was hard enough to be so old when John was born. But I can imagine the thoughts that must have run through her mind when he took the vow of the Nazarite and stopped cutting his hair. When he refused to eat anything but locusts and honey, she probably worried he wasn't getting enough to eat. And when he started sleeping out in the wilderness, where it could get so cold at night, I'll bet, like any other mother, she was convinced he would catch pneumonia. I can almost see her chasing behind him and calling out, "Now, John, please pay more attention to what you're eating, dear. Take this little cake I've fixed when you go, and *do* cover up at night! I just can't understand why you have to live out in the desert like that. I do worry about you so!" But she let him go. Although his life would end with his head on a king's platter, his mother, Elizabeth, enabled him to become the man God had created him to be. And John became the voice, crying in the wilderness, which prepared the way for the Messiah.

I had some feelings like Elizabeth's when I took Jonathan to the first grade. I wrote in my journal that day:

Well, we did it Lord—You and I took Jonathan to school this morning, so spick-and-span he messed up his hair after he got out of the car, so he'd feel more like himself. I smiled as I remembered his prayer last night. "Lord, please help me not to disobey, so I won't get my hand squeezed hard." And I was silently praying the same kind of prayer. "Lord, help him keep his arms and legs still enough to sit at a desk. And please don't let him be the first one to step out of line, to be made the example of!" I felt such a sense of loss as I watched him taking his seat this morning. Maybe I am grieving for his childhood as I saw the notepads and the books that spoke of serious business. Maybe the loss I feel is some tearing asunder of an invisible heartstring that should be torn, but leaves a wound nevertheless. He just won't be needing me quite the same again. I felt a quiet exchange taking place as his teacher kindly but firmly motioned me to leave. "Give her wisdom, Lord. And love." It helped to see I wasn't the only mother with tears in my eyes.

Our silent looks to one another spoke volumes. Thank You for the kind of love that hurts a little bit, because that's one of the ways I know it's deep and real and precious. And thank You that Lucian has locked his keys in his car today, so I'll have to go by his office. Maybe he's having some heart pangs, too.

It isn't always easy letting go, but it's so important if we are to be the kind of encouragers who enable life to grow.

Rita has had to learn this principle in her relationship with her husband as well. She has had to love him enough to let him go through a mid-life crisis that has been pretty messy for everyone. I met Rita at an out-of-town conference, and the tale she told me was pretty hair-raising, but also fairly classic. Her husband was in the process of reevaluating every area of his life. He had questions about his career. He had questions about his priorities. He wondered if he wanted to be married and if he wanted to be a father to their four children. He questioned his faith. He struggled to meet his own needs and wondered if these needs could possibly fit into a family structure. He was trying on a new life-style. He was vigorously exercising and dieting, and he had even bought a new sports car. He had also found a girl friend, and the ultimate came for Rita when that girl friend confronted her one day at the grocery store. They hashed out the whole situation right over the frozen broccoli. Rita said she hasn't been able to eat broccoli ever since. But she has persevered with her husband in a remarkable way. And she has encouraged him in spite of everything. "A lot of good has come out of this, really," she said to me. "Not only has my faith in God increased as I've learned to depend on Him more, but I have also seen many of my own shortcomings, and I have found myself in the process. If Dick hadn't left home, I probably never would have become a real woman. It's so much easier not to. But now that I see who I am, why should I throw away a lifetime, just because my husband has gone a little crazy? He'll work it through. I believe in him. And I love him. A lot of people keep telling me to go ahead and get a divorce, but why should I let my pride get in the way at this point? We have had a good marriage, and we have a strong foundation. I'm drawing on that now, along with the Lord." Rita became strong. She took her turn as the steadying force in the marriage, while her husband was faltering and buffeted about by his inner doubts. I felt encouraged, just talking to her.

But women don't have to have traumas in life to encourage. Hundreds of opportunities to cheer someone along his way face us each week. The last time I grocery shopped, I overheard a lady telling the young stock clerk in the produce department, "It is such a pleasure to come into your section of the store. The fruits and vegetables are always lined up so neatly and attractively. You do such a good job." The young man literally beamed with pleasure. Someone had noticed. Someone thought he was doing well. As he thanked the lady he absentmindedly picked up an apple and began to polish it. She made his day, and it hadn't taken her a minute. Life isn't easy, but a woman can make it a lot more bearable when she uses the power God has given her to encourage. It's one of the ways she mothers mankind.

Today women face a challenge, as never before, to use the gifts God has given us to counsel, to serve, to comfort, and to encourage. The world cries out for the feminine touch. We can greet this challenge with courage and expectancy, determined to try to change the course of history with our love. Or we can choose to turn our backs on these gifts and instead use our energies to grab for the world's kind of power. The same power God used to hurl together a universe is at the center of a woman's love. I pray that we will choose to use it for good. God created women for such an hour in history.

> Don't crowd me.
> I need room to grow,
> to stretch my wings,
> breathe deep and slow,
> to look about,
> to think things through;
> don't hem me in,
> don't block the view.

Don't push me;
I need time to grow,
to savor life from day
to day; freedom to go
at my own pace;
leisure to live more thoroughly,
unherded and unhurried, please;
just let me BE.

Don't stalk me.
Follow where He leads
though it may mean
another path, one needs
one single aim in life:
follow well, work hard,
obedient and faithful. So
Go!—after God.

RUTH GRAHAM

9

Women at Work

But how are women to use these attributes of counseling, helping, comforting, and encouraging out in the world? How can a woman be a helper and a mother to mankind in the working world?

When I arrived a little early for the meeting, the sun had already set, and as I looked out the windows of the second-story room I could see the stars twinkling in the clear winter night. The radiator clanked noisily, and the air was heavy with the stuffiness of windows long shut tight against the wind. Pat sat stiffly at the head of the table, her lips pursed tightly as she passed a formal agenda around to her board members. Her eyes glanced at the clock on the wall, and she frowned slightly at the men she saw chatting amiably in the hall outside the room. It was two minutes past the hour the meeting should have started, and Pat seemed uncomfortable. She now faced her first experience as board chairman and she took her job very seriously, much too seriously, although admittedly she held an important position. As she began the meeting a hushed, unpleasant silence enveloped the room. I noticed once Pat was in charge no one felt the freedom to smile or insert humorous barbs into the business discussion. She barreled through the agenda, oblivious to the personalities of those around her, asking questions about the committee reports in such a sterile manner that even the most capable members appeared somewhat inadequate, as though they had not met Pat's standards of perfection. Yet when anyone questioned her suggestions, she immediately reacted defensively, especially if one of the men challenged her ideas.

As I tried to look at her objectively I could see she felt tired. In spite of her fresh makeup, I saw deep circles under her eyes. She had come to the meeting straight from work. Probably she skipped dinner. There was no joy about her and consequently no joy in the interactions taking place around her. She did not smile once the entire evening. I wondered if the others also wanted to get away as badly as I did. The committee was made up of a great group of people. We could have really enjoyed our work together as we transacted the business, if Pat had allowed us to. It was such a shame. I knew Pat socially. Ordinarily she was fun and warm, easy to know. I wondered why she did not bring those same characteristics into her position of leadership. Was it having the men there that intimidated her? Why did she seem to feel she must be so stern in order to be professional?

Watching her reminded me of one of my conversations with a former student, Dana, who is now an attorney in a large city. Darkly beautiful and very feminine, she had never lacked boyfriends. But she told me some of the pressures she felt in her profession worked against that femininity. She spoke of feeling she must be masculinely aggressive in the courtroom, dressing in a severe, no-nonsense manner when she worked, curbing her natural softness in order to effectively challenge the male attorneys before a judge and jury. Yet in a characteristically feminine way, she found herself drawn to those cases that helped the helpless. She enjoyed her role as an advocate. But only now was she beginning to feel confident enough to wear a frilly blouse beneath her tailored suits and to relax enough to smile when she argued a point. Only now was she beginning to enjoy her femininity within the context of her profession.

With the growing number of women joining the work force on a full-time basis each year, a professional woman faces the important task of seeing how she can use her unique gifts on a professional level, and she needs to find models for how a woman can be the helper, comforter, encourager, and counselor in positions that have traditionally been occupied by men.

Of the many students in that typical middle-class neighborhood high school in which I taught over a decade ago, I have kept up with only four of them. Dana is one. The paths which these four women have taken signal a direction more and more women will be following in the years ahead. It is imperative women learn how to be feminine in their professions.

Of the four who turned thirty this year, only one of them is a traditional wife and mother. Petite and dark-haired Virginia, an accomplished flutist who taught music for several years in the public schools, has married a doctor and stays home with their young child. She is frequently asked to play her flute at church on Sundays. Studious, keen-minded Marietta, however, has followed her dream down another road. She was awarded a scholarship to medical school and is currently in a pediatrics residency in one of the finest programs in the country. Married to a fellow resident, she enclosed a picture of their infant daughter in her last Christmas card. She and her husband plan to practice medicine in his native country, Kenya, following the completion of their training.

Grawin is the fourth. Quiet, sensitive, and artistic, she would secretly slip her beautiful poems into my desk drawer at the front of the room when she was in the tenth grade, or she might tack them on the end of a class assignment. Now married and trained as a psychiatric nurse, she sent me a package recently. When I opened it, I discovered a copy of her first book of poetry. Surely it was one of the finest gifts an old teacher could ever receive. Women like Grawin, Dana, Marietta, and Virginia are coming into their own, discovering multiple gifts and talents that have long been submerged below the surface of awareness for the majority of us, taking the time to discover these gifts, to develop them, and to exercise these talents, in addition to being wives and mothers. They are working out individual systems that allow them to do both.

I watched a busy pediatrician in operation, behind the scenes, when we spent one afternoon out at the Claxton's farm. Martha Ann has found a method that works for her, allowing her to be a professional, a wife, and a mother. Her husband, Porter, is a thoracic surgeon, and he was on duty that day. He arrived just in time to sit down to a country feast of succulent fried chicken, cucumbers and tomatoes, fresh corn that Martha Ann had cut off the cob, and green beans from their garden. She brought in biscuits and homemade jam she had put up herself the summer before, and as I watched her serving the fourteen of us who sat at her table it was hard to remember she was also a busy doctor three days a week.

I recalled the day Jonathan had split open his chin, and I had rushed him, bleeding all over both of us, into her office. Martha Ann had done a masterful job. Beginning by comforting me, she had said, "I'll bet you're feeling just terrible about this." That comment released my false guilt and calmed me down. "No mother can be everywhere at once," she reassuringly commented and then related a similar accident that had happened to one of her five children. Since she was a mother in addition to being a pediatrician, she knew how I was feeling. She also knew that a hysterical mother was not what her patient needed at that moment, and she was calming me down so I could be strong for Jonathan once more, giving him the comfort and encouragement to face the ordeal of having stitches. Soon everything was going smoothly. Only after the tears were dry, the balloon for good behavior had been passed out, and she had reassured me the scar would be hardly noticeable, did she counsel us both about how we could avoid such an accident in the future. Martha Ann's feminine gifts combined with her outstanding medical expertise formed an unbeatable combination.

But as I watched her in her home, with her husband and children, I saw another side of her. Her two daughters had helped prepare our meal and quietly and efficiently helped her clean up. Each child in the family seemed to have a wide assortment of tacitly accepted responsibilities. I could see they also had a lot of freedom and a lot of fun together. After lunch we all walked down the hill to the barn, where a small but varied assortment of animals lived. My children were enchanted. Although the barnyard chores didn't appear to be overwhelming, they were regular. The cows had to be milked and the eggs gathered every day. Each member of the family had one day of the week when he did the chores. This particular day belonged to Porter, and regardless of the fact he was on hospital duty, he managed to sandwich them all in.

I could see that Martha Ann was also a good mother. She let a lot of the little things go by the way, but she never missed keeping a close eye on the important issues regarding her children. They all seemed to get along well together. There was a genuine family community spirit among them. They helped one another and also helped Martha Ann care for her mother, who had come to live with them. Although I was used to seeing Martha Ann dressed in her white laboratory coat or in a pretty party dress at some social gathering, she seemed equally at home in her blue jeans. There was a naturalness about her. She obviously loved her life; she loved her family; and she felt very much at home with herself.

As we returned home from the barn, the earthy smell of the farm animals clinging to our hands and our clothes, I saw a dark blue pickup truck climbing the road that led to the house. A young teenage couple followed us into the kitchen, the baby-faced mother carrying a whimpering child, wrapped in a quilt in her arms. I sat on the stool at the large work area in the middle of Martha Ann's country kitchen and silently watched her professionally checking over the baby. She quickly sent one of her children to the bedroom for her stethoscope. Soon the couple and their child were on their way, the young mother relieved and clutching a prescription in one hand.

"Does this happen very often?" I asked, wondering how she could possibly handle this kind of interruption in addition to her other responsibilities.

"Not very often," she replied. "I was just being neighborly. Last year their daddy helped Porter cut the hay from the back field and mend the barn. This was one way I could say thank-you."

I was pretty awed. That afternoon I had watched Martha Ann as a mother and as a wife to a busy husband. I had seen her entertain friends, and I had observed her as a professional. She handled each task un-self-consciously and with grace, shifting gears noiselessly and taking each role as it came, bringing her most feminine qualities as a helper, a comforter, an encourager, and a counselor into every situation. Most amazing of all to me, however, was that for all her excellence, she had not been in the least intimidating to be around. It had been a joy to watch her work in each of her capacities.

Finding a balance like this is a hard fought battle. It doesn't come all by itself, and it requires a lot of self-honesty and a constant evaluation of priorities. I have been experiencing some of the tension of finding a system for myself as I have written this book, allowing myself to be a professional as well as a good wife and mother.

Until very recently I had no idea I would ever be a writer. I am a notoriously poor letter writer; and although I have a background in English, my only other writing experience consists of annual Christmas letters to our friends, and some sporadic scribbling in a private journal, when I want to sort out my thoughts. So when a friend challenged me to write some sample chapters about the comparison between the Holy Spirit and the feminine and to send them to a publisher, I worked on them only because I believed I had something important to say. When I received a contract for my material, I was speechless. They liked it. They said they wanted more of it. I felt as though I had been asked to play "Rhapsody in Blue" at Carnegie Hall, and I had never had a piano lesson. Although I was exhilarated by the discovery of a new gift, panic soon set in. After all, I was only a housewife in a small town. I had two elementary-school children. My husband's schedule was already full. My own calendar contained many speaking engagements. How would I ever write a book? I felt so inadequate and vulnerable. What if I failed? What if nobody liked what I wrote? I faced so many hours of research, composing, editing, rewriting. But then again, what if I succeeded? That would mean I would have to make all sorts of new, hard decisions about my priorities. I felt torn. I believed in what I wanted to say, but I feared saying it. I couldn't write a word for five months after I signed my contract.

Finally I called my friend Bob, who has written ten books and is one of the editors of our local newspaper.

"Tell me how to write a book!" I begged. "Is there some course I can quickly take?"

"Each writer is different," Bob answered. "Every author must find his own method. I've used a different system for each one of my books. At this point a course would only confuse you. Just start writing, and do the best you can by your family. They'll survive. Before you know it, you'll be working on the next one."

"The next one!" I shuddered. I couldn't see how I was going to do *this* one. But when I finally began to write, I loved it. I loved working with words; I loved the intimacy of feeling as if the reader and I were having a cozy chat together in my study, getting to know each other so well I didn't need to feel obliged to pick up my scattered papers and books or my dirty coffee cup. And I loved discovering I could do something I never before imagined I could do. Some nights I got up before dawn with a new idea. There have been days of sitting alone with my thoughts, when nothing would come at all. The family has eaten out a lot more than usual, and I'll admit I edited a chapter or two while I watched Jonathan play baseball. But I was about halfway through the manuscript when I realized what was happening to me. Writing about being a helper, a comforter, an encourager, and a counselor put me more closely in touch with my own capacities in these areas. I realized, as the author, I was trying to do all those things for my reader. I instinctively brought my feminine gifts into my profession, and as I did I felt more pleased with the results and with myself. I realized my highest priority for my book was for the women who read it to feel better about themselves, when they had finished, stimulated to discover how they could be the best women possible in their own unique situations. I also noticed that when the work went well, I was a better wife and mother.

Iva Stafford summed up my feelings beautifully one day when she saw my husband in his office. "My head may belong to my business," she said. "But my heart always belongs to my family." Iva held a position as the president of an aeronautical corporation before she died last year, from lung cancer. Lucian described her as one of the most feminine women he has ever met. Although she flew all over the world, negotiating multimillion-dollar contracts, her main interest remained in the people with whom she came in contact. A tall and very bright woman, she had a commanding physical presence and was very competent in her profession. Iva did her job well and had a reputation for working hard at negotiations. Although many men worked under her leadership, every one of them both respected and loved her. I wonder how many corporation presidents that could be said about? Once when she failed to receive an important contract, she expressed much more concern for the future of her employees than for the prestige of her company. And she was as committed to the well-being of her family as she was to her co-workers. She wed her expertise in the business world with her feminine gifts, both at work and in the home, where she applied organizational skills to make life run more smoothly. It worked. Even as she excelled as a corporation president she also excelled as a woman.

I also had the pleasure of watching my own mother use her feminine gifts in a professional context. The day I slipped into the large auditorium to watch her sitting on a school board that made decisions for one of the largest school systems in the country, she did not see me come in. The television lights glared on her face, and I could hear the cameras whirring as I listened to the heated debate over a union dispute. The meeting would more than likely last for hours, and each word the board members uttered was beamed into the living rooms of their constituents. In spite of the pressure, the heat of the lights, and the length of the meeting, my mother still looked fresh. I had never before noticed so vividly how pretty she is. Although she radiated a distinctly professional air, she also wore a dress in her best color. It gave her a softness, and she looked very much the lady that she is. Her words held an unyielding strength, but she was not overbearing. She merely let her competence speak for itself. Obviously she had done her homework well and knew her topic. The questions she asked revealed the depth of her keen mind. She saw no need to flaunt her expertise. And she had a wonderfully diplomatic way of making a point. As I watched her I realized with surprise that my mother was a marvelous politician—and a feminine one. She seemed to have a way of intuitively picking out the contradictions in an argument and of seeing the more human ramifications of a decision. I could see that although the men on the board didn't always agree with her, they had come to listen carefully to her perceptions. She brought her feminine wisdom into her professional capacity and did it in a lovely manner. I felt so proud to be her daughter.

As women become more accepted in the professions and as we come to feel more comfortable in them, we will feel more freedom to bring our feminine gifts into these jobs. This will enable us to integrate our separate roles into a way of being—a way of being a woman—whether at the office at nine, with our children at five, out with friends at eight, or in the bedroom with our husbands at eleven. Women will begin to feel less fragmented and more whole, like Martha Ann, shifting gears with confidence and grace because we are comfortable with the many facets of our lives and have found the freedom to express them all.

10

Women in the Church

Just as women need to bring their gifts into the professional world as helpers, counselors, comforters, and encouragers, they must also have the freedom to exercise these gifts within the church, where in many instances, women are not being used in the capacities for which they have been uniquely gifted.

I discovered some problems along these lines not too long after I became a Christian. Several months after I began attending church once more, I met Eddie. He called himself a completed Jew and said he knew Jesus as his Messiah. Eddie took me alongside to feed me the spiritual food that enables spiritual babes to grow, teaching me discipline about reading my Bible and teaching me how to pray. Eddie said you could pray anywhere, and I noticed he prayed on the tennis court, if he felt like it, even with his eyes open. He answered hundreds of my questions, never laughing at the most elementary or criticizing the most heretical. He merely pointed me back to God's owners' manual—the Bible—for all my answers. Eddie showed me that God had created me for a purpose and had equipped each of us with special gifts He wanted us to use to accomplish His work in the world. He encouraged me to ask God to reveal my gifts and to trust Him to use me just as He had once used His disciples.

As I began reading my Bible I saw that women were clearly portrayed as spiritual equals with men and that the gifts the Holy Spirit brought at Penetecost were given regardless of sex. The prophet Joel wrote, ". . . I will pour out my spirit on all flesh; your sons and your daughters shall prophesy, your old men shall dream dreams, and your young men shall see visions. Even upon the menservants and maidservants in those days, I will pour out my spirit" (Joel 2:28, 29). I read that Paul said, "For as many of you as were baptized into Christ have put on Christ. There is neither Jew nor Greek, there is neither slave nor free, there is neither male nor female; for you are all one in Christ Jesus" (Galatians 3:27, 28).

As I dug into the Old Testament I found that Hebrew women had enjoyed a substantially elevated position, compared with the women of the nations surrounding Israel. Israelite law protected women, giving them rights and freedom unknown in ancient times. Many women in the Old Testament were greatly admired. Sarah was honored for her faith; Esther and Ruth were revered, with entire books of the Bible recounting their hearts for God; and even Rahab, a harlot, was in the lineage of Jesus because of her courage. Perhaps most striking was the story of Deborah, found in Judges 4 and 5. A remarkably gifted woman, called of God to minister to His people, Deborah not only held authority as a prophetess, but also as the judge of Israel. She led the troops into battle against the Canaanites, interpreted the law, spoke God's word to the people, wrote poetry, and kept house for her husband, Lapidoth, all at the same time. Although the Bible mentions no natural children, it calls her the mother of Israel, and under her rule Israel enjoyed forty years of peace. She was pretty impressive.

Reading in the New Testament, I also saw that Jesus greatly respected women. He had the kind of warm, intimate relationship with them unheard of in that day. Many women were prominent in the activities of the early church, ministering, teaching, and holding positions of spiritual influence. Anna was a prophetess; Mary Magdalene was the first to see the risen Christ, carrying the news to the disciples; Priscilla was an instructor; and Paul entrusted Phoebe, a deaconess and fellow worker with Paul, with his important letter to the church at Rome, where she traveled on a business trip.

At the same time, Paul states in 1 Corinthians 14:34: "The women should keep silence in the churches. For they are not permitted to speak but should be subordinate, as even the law says," and in 1 Timothy 2:11-14: "Let a woman learn in silence with all submissiveness. I permit no woman to teach or to have authority over men; she is to keep silent. For Adam was formed first, then Eve; and Adam was not deceived, but the woman was deceived...."
Apparently some women were interrupting the services, speaking in

tongues in a disorderly fashion and in general abusing their free position in Christ by exercising their authority over the authority of men, not operating under an order of leadership. But in exhorting these women who were out of order, I wondered if Paul was exhorting every woman for the rest of all time to keep silent in every service of worship. Apparently not, for women who were in order prayed aloud, prophesied, taught men, and were respected members of the early church, as long as they exhibited that servant attitude Christ exhorted all Christians to have one to another, male and female.

From all I could tell, it seemed there should exist plenty of room within the church for women to function as talented and successful individuals, using their gifts creatively. The church was founded on love. What better place for the feminine need to be warm, nurturing, and to establish strong relationships? The entire structure seemed a wonderful container in which both men and women could develop the masculine and the feminine components in all of us, working side by side as we learned how to love one another. I envisioned women being called upon to exercise their gifts in cooperation with men who had the same gifts, the whole church working together as smoothly as the body of a well-trained athlete. I was very idealistic.

When I discovered I had a teaching gift, administrative gifts, perhaps even a mini gift in evangelism, however, and not the more traditionally feminine gifts of helps and mercy, I discovered that using my gifts put me in the middle of a controversy, in the evangelical church, regarding the role of women. At the heart of the matter seemed to lie a definition of the Greek word *kephale,* or "head," as well as the definition of another controversial word: *submission.* These were difficult concepts to sort out, and I didn't know what to do about using my gifts. I certainly didn't want to put on a Christian mask just as I was becoming convinced for the very first time that God made me the way He did for a reason. It seemed my job to discover what that reason was.

So I began to teach the Bible, and my husband supported me. One thing led to another, and what started as a small lecture series for twenty women tripled in size by the end of the first six weeks. By the end of the year, it had multiplied tenfold. Soon The Storehouse was born, an interdenominational ministry for women. I began speaking at conferences, where at first I was on safe ground. I taught women, and no one objected to that. But then someone pointed out to me that Paul had instructed the older women to teach the younger women, and not the other way around. That brought my first problem. I was a younger woman. A lot of grandmothers came to my class. What did Paul mean by *old?* Was he referring to spiritual or to physical maturity? I received a letter from a very sincere young woman who said, "From my study, I honestly do not see where women are called to be teachers, except in a very narrow sense. I would not go so far as to say that I didn't learn from your teaching, because I did, but I would have been much more comfortable seeing an elderly woman. There are so many areas other than teaching women that we younger ladies can be involved in." I felt frustrated, and I wanted to write her back, "I would love to feel more comfortable, too. It's not easy getting up to speak in front of a group of women. But God has called me to teach, not to feel comfortable."

I noticed that the churches encouraged women to teach children, however, but now I had another problem. I needed to know when a child became a man, because I was beginning to speak on some college campuses, and some churches feel the Bible forbids women to teach men. Was a college-aged man too old for me to teach? Or was it all right as long as he was still in school, but not all right if he had a job? No one seemed to be able to give me a definitive answer.

My problems multiplied. Now the lectures for The Storehouse were on tape, and the women took their tapes home. Soon the first husband appeared at the Bible study. It seemed very rude to ask him to leave because I was not supposed to teach men, so I let him stay. To make matters worse, the tapes were occasionally aired on the conference hour of the local religious radio station, and of course men listened, too. There was no way I could control that, and as many men as women wrote for copies of the tapes they had heard.

The problem of how to use my gifts became intensified when I was next asked to speak at a Sunday-morning worship service. The first time this happened I turned down the pastor's request on the grounds women were to keep silent in the churches. I told him I would gladly speak on a Sunday or Wednesday evening, since those were not official worship services, but his church did not have services on Sunday and Wednesday nights. The second invitation I accepted, however, reasoning that since the spiritual leader—the pastor—had asked me to speak, I would teach under his authority. When I arrived, we discussed where I would stand to speak. If I stood in the pulpit, would it appear I was exercising too much authority? If I stood on the level of the congregation, as a layman, would that be more appropriate? What if they couldn't see me? I'm not very tall. Was it all right for me, as a woman, to stand in a subordinate pulpit instead of the main one? Did it really make any difference at all where I stood? Wasn't what I had to say really more important?

What can a woman of God do when she has a gift God commands her to use and He is changing lives through it, but her gift is controversial? Remembering the story Jesus told about the servant who buried his talent and was judged severely for the mismanagement of all God had given him, I have persevered. If the church does not hesitate to send a woman to evangelize on a foreign field, why is she sometimes not permitted to teach a mixed Sunday-school class? Somewhere in the midst of the controversy, is church missing the substance of what the Bible teaches about women, and is it losing these women? The United Methodist Church, of which I am a member, recently conducted a survey about women's attitudes toward the church, and they discovered a vast majority of women are not going to their pastors for help in times of crisis. Right now a lot of women face crisis and need the church as never before, to undergird us, to listen to us, and to encourage us to find and to use our gifts, in order that the whole Body of Christ may be strengthened.

I have seen what can happen when a woman takes over a church, exercising the wrong kind of authority, weakening the fellowship, and causing the kind of dissension only a woman can cause. I believe Paul wrote to that type of woman in 1 Corinthians. But scores of other women wish to serve the church in ways other than putting macaroni and cheese on the plastic trays at the church-night supper or embroidering fine linen altar scarves, as important as these tasks are. A woman who is gifted by God and is effective in His service should not be barred from using her gift. Perhaps the time has come for the entire Body of Christ to prayerfully reexamine the role of women from God's perspective, laying aside our divisiveness and our fears, to search out new and creative ways in which women can function in the church.

Women have traditionally been the helpers in the church and over the centuries have served well in this function. We make the casseroles for the covered-dish suppers, work behind the scenes rolling bandages for the sick, sew layettes for the poor, and make hundreds of telephone calls to assure good participation in all the fund-raising projects. We make the draperies for the fellowship hall and polish the candlesticks. We also lead the children's choir, change diapers in the nursery, teach Vacation Bible School, cut up the bread for communion, and arrange the flowers for the sanctuary on Sunday morning. We come to the christenings, weddings, and the funerals that are part of the life of the church and faithfully attend the prayer meetings and choir rehearsals. We have been wonderful nurturers, counselors, and encouragers, especially to the youth of the church.

But in other areas women could function equally well, given the opportunity. I would love to see each church develop a core group of women to visit the sick and the bereaved, on a regular basis, on behalf of the church. They could offer the kind of comfort only a woman can bring, in addition to the often hurried service a busy pastor has to provide because there is no one to help him with his visitation responsibilities. I can see how helpful it would be for him to train and assign a woman to follow up each family who has had a death, coming back to visit in the weeks that follow the funeral, checking on the family, listening to their grief, and staying beside them as they work through that long process. Women have a warmth, concern, and an empathetic understanding that the church could use so much more creatively.

I would also like to see at least one woman on every church committee. If the feminine point of view is essential in arriving at a total picture on any issue and women have been created to complement the masculine side of life, logically, both perspectives should receive a chance to influence decisions that affect the life of the whole Body. Having the counsel of a mature Christian woman can only add to the effectiveness of any committee. Furthermore women discern needs the more rational masculine mind sometimes misses, and we adeptly advocate on behalf of these needs. The church should provide a place where women can exercise these gifts in an appropriate manner.

I can also see the value of a group of specially trained women to assist the pastor with his counseling duties, working beside him in ministry to church members in crisis. The feminine perspective can aid in marriage counseling, in problems with teenagers, and with the depression that often faces women who are single, divorced, or widowed. The majority of parishioners who come to their pastors for counseling are women, and they could be greatly helped by the active listening of another woman, in addition to the spiritual guidance of their pastor.

Women compose half the Body of Christ, and the church must begin using all its parts at full capacity, if it would become the trailblazer, for which it has the potential in the new era dawning between the sexes. After all, God created us male and female in the first place, and to His Body Christ gave the blueprint for how we are to live together in love. Will we miss this opportunity to lead because we are embattled in the intricacies of the meaning of Greek words, instead of searching to expand our vision of God's revelation? God's creation continues, and I believe He means to build it upon the rock of His church, instead of the sands of these shifting times. The church must search for new ways to use God's women, building up a stronger Body of Christ, if it is to be all that it is meant to be in this age.

Part III

When We Uncover Our Faces

LORD, shall we not bring these gifts to Your service?
Shall we not bring to Your service all our powers
For life, for dignity, grace and order...?

T. S. ELIOT
"Choruses from 'The Rock'"

11

The Wicked Witch

Power is a gift from God, and He has given all of us a measure of it to enable us to subdue the earth. Yet power easily gets out of hand when it is never given limits or subdued within us. When a woman uses the power of her femininity for her own selfish ends, she becomes ineffective. The same powerful movement of water that, when harnessed, produces electricity also floods, leaving death and destruction in its path.

Once when the children and I were driving across town in rush-hour traffic, they got bored and decided to play house. "You be the baby, and I'll be the mommy," I heard Rebecca saying to Jonathan as I quietly listened to discover what kind of example I was setting for my daughter. I congratulated myself on my success as I heard her using all sorts of tender, endearing phrases with her imaginary baby. But suddenly, Rebecca let out a great roar, which precipitated fierce pretend crying from her brother.

"What in the world, Rebecca?" I couldn't resist asking.

"Oh, don't you know?" she said. "The mommy is also a witch."

I had been revealed all right, pricked by the thorns on that rose bush of my femininity and forced to look upon the dark side of the power in a woman's love.

That great life force that surges through a woman can as easily be used to suffocate, to devour, and to manipulate as it can be used to comfort, to encourage, and to serve. Our power to counsel and to strengthen can instantly turn into a sword that belittles and misadvises. Within every woman lies a wicked witch, working against her best efforts to become a mother to the living and a helper of mankind. The witch can erupt quite suddenly, as she does at my house, generally appearing early in the morning, especially on days we're running late, or as she did with my friend Carol—one Thanksgiving

Day she found herself throwing a frozen turkey across the room at her husband.

A small group of us sat around Ruth's dining-room table, discussing this very issue. Margaret piped up honestly and said, "Remember when you were a little girl, and you wanted something from your father? I remember once I wanted a nickel. I must have been about five. Dad said I couldn't have it, so I threw myself on the floor, in a tantrum, grazing my head slightly on the coffee table. I howled as though I were dying. Dad rushed over in concern, solicitously picked me up, and said, 'Now, now, Margaret. Don't cry. If you'll stop crying, Daddy will give you a quarter.'" We all exploded with laughter. Margaret had come out twenty cents ahead by using her feminine wiles. But we also agreed we despised this kind of behavior in our daughters.

It reminded me of the time I had parked in a NO-PARKING area, to run inside a store and make a quick delivery. When I returned, not only would my car not start, but a policeman was walking toward me. I was stuck. When he drew up to the window to begin writing out my ticket, I quickly flipped the ignition over to show him my car wouldn't start.

"What's the matter, lady?" he asked, now diverted from writing the ticket.

"I don't know, sir," I answered in my most helpless voice. "It's just broken, I guess." And it worked. I didn't get a ticket. Had I tried that on a female officer, I probably would have been given two tickets!

Every woman alive knows how to play these games. We keep our motives a secret, say no when we mean yes, and seductively use our power to get our way, manipulating husbands, sons, and bosses into giving us what we want by making it look as if they had the idea all along. But it is deceptive and dishonest. It is also sin. When the wicked witch on the inside, dresses up as the charming belle on the outside, we act like Scarlett O'Hara—the antithesis of what God means for us to be as women.

Many authorities on women believe this manipulative form of power comes from centuries of powerlessness. They suggest when women have more power of our own in the world, we will not use it underhandedly—that when we recognize our own power, we will stop trying to live our lives through our husbands and sons, driving them to fulfill our ambitions instead of their own. There is some truth here. But I think the problem lies deeper than this.

A basic core of selfishness and egocentricity resides in all of us, no matter how much or how little power we have. The Bible calls it our sin nature; psychology calls it our shadow or our id; anthropologists speak of our survival animal instinct. But whatever you want to call it, we must deal with it. We must decide what we will do with our power; how we will use it; and who it will serve.

We've all met the women who serve from a sense of duty, instead of from the heart. They often sigh deeply, somewhere in the back of the kitchen. Their attitude seems to be, "I'm going to serve you, if it kills me, which it probably will, so you'd better appreciate it properly!" These martyrs make everybody feel guilty and then wonder why everyone leaves as soon as possible. After all, "Look what I do for them! How ungrateful they are!"

There are those of us who serve manipulatively. Rushing in to help, unasked, we brush off efficient hands in smug satisfaction and smile sweetly as our attitude says, "Now that I have done all this for you, I expect you to do something for me." We ingratiate ourselves to others in order to control them and then feel abandoned and unloved when we don't get what we want in return.

Some also selfishly help individuals who should be helping themselves, because helping meets a need to be needed. The zealous woman of this sort only feels good when she helps, so she may "mother" her husband in an overly solicitous way that undermines his manhood or never gives someone else a chance to be in charge. How much of this kind of helping is done in the name of Christianity!

Or there are the *smother mothers,* who instead of encouraging new growth, smother with their comfort, like a feather bed on a hot summer night. "I don't want you to be hurt by life," they say, "so I won't let you live it. I want you to be comfortable, and life isn't always comfortable, so I will protect you from it." In their well-meaning way, they stifle maturity, clipping grownup wings, which are meant to be used for flying; meeting needs that no longer need meeting; still shoving the worm down the throats of those who should be out finding worms or mates or nests of their own.

Or finally there are the *god mothers,* who play God in the lives of those around them. All-knowing, all-loving, all-sufficient, they naturally see exactly what is best for everyone, and expect others to follow their directions, all the while praising them and giving adoration for all they do. Instead of challenging others to seek God's purpose for their lives and letting Him be God, they usurp His position and then wonder why those they love never seem to want a relationship with God for themselves.

How often we fall into one or more of these ugly categories. There have been times I have been every one of them. We have a responsibility to come to terms with this shadowy side of ourselves, if we want to have the positive side of our power at our disposal. Robert Johnson says, in his marvelous little book *She,* that women have two valuable items: a lamp, with which we can shed the light of our insight, and a knife, with which we can impale with those deadly looks and devastating remarks we all use at times, skewering the very ones we love with an angry flow of words. Choosing whether we use the lamp or the knife in any situation is one of a woman's greatest responsibilities, and it is a choice we all face many times each day.

Perhaps the most vulnerable time for any of us is when we first recognize our power. If we have long had feelings of low self-esteem, as many women have, at this point we can become prideful and dangerously inflated. It is not an accident that Jesus was propelled by the Holy Spirit into the wilderness, where Satan tempted Him and the Father tested Him, immediately after He was empowered for His unique mission here on earth. Upon first recognizing our power as God's women, we, too, can expect to be tested and tempted, tried in a refiner's fire to see how we will come through. And the wicked witch will be there, whispering in our ears, "Use the power for yourself. You deserve it." But improperly used power will turn us into the kind of helpers who become hindrances and into mothers who devour.

Perhaps the most graphic literary picture of a woman who turned into a wicked witch is found in the story of Jezebel. We can learn much from her in this area of how to use our power. The story of her life starkly reminds us of what can happen to a woman who misuses her power. Through it, God sends an important message to those of us who are discovering our power as women. Her story was written for such a time as this.

When we think of Jezebel, we usually think of a harlot with a painted face. That's how she ended her life, but not how she began it. Most people consumed by their own power are remembered for their falls. The Bible indicates that Jezebel started out as a golden girl, however. Endowed with an abundance of natural gifts and talents, she was beautiful, very intelligent, and came from an important family. The Bible suggests she possessed a powerful charisma that drew people to her. She had a great talent for influencing others; and it is not surprising, with all these gifts, she became the bride of the most powerful man in the land: King Ahab. Jezebel had all the ingredients of a queen, and when she became queen, the power of her position was added to all her other attributes. How would she use all that power?

The meaning of a biblical figure's name is often significant, indicative of his or her inner character. Jezebel's name meant "chaste." God apparently gifted Jezebel with all this power so she could use it to serve Him, wisely and virtuously serving His people as their queen. But Jezebel had another heritage working within her, as well, which warred with her heritage from God. The Bible says she was the daughter of the high priest of Baal, the high priest of evil; and Jezebel chose to identify with her earthly heritage, instead of her heavenly one. She chose to use the knife, instead of the lamp. She chose to serve her own selfish desires, instead of God, and it was the beginning of her destruction.

Jezebel became obsessed with power. It was not enough merely to be the queen. She wanted also to be the king. She wanted to be all-powerful. She wanted to be God. This same desire led the most beautiful angel of light, Lucifer, to war against God and to be banished from heaven. The desire for such power caused God to banish Adam and Eve from Eden and caused Jezebel, the one created to be chaste, to become the harlot of Israel. Her great potential as a helper and a wise counselor, advocating for good instead of evil, became destructive and devouring, sowing death all around her, until she eventually destroyed herself.

First Jezebel overpowered her husband, Ahab. Soon she had become the ruler of Israel, working through his position to achieve her own ends. Then she drove out God's prophets and replaced them with the prophets of Baal. The moral fiber of the nation began to deteriorate. Ahab turned away from God becoming weak and ineffective, cut off from his capacity to love by the ruthless power lust of his wife. His feminine wellspring, his wife, had become polluted by her greed for power. The people turned from God as well, and the land became barren and sterile. A serious drought and a famine affected both the land and the heart of Israel. Ahab and Jezebel produced evil offspring, the most wicked of which, naturally, was their daughter. But perhaps worst of all, Jezebel did all this under the guise of religion. Assuming the role of a prophetess, she used her own power to seduce the minds of the people away from God.

Finally a day of reckoning came for Jezebel. It always comes. God declared to Jehu, "And you shall strike down the house of Ahab, your master, that I may avenge on Jezebel the blood of my servants the prophets, and the blood of all the servants of the Lord. For the whole house of Ahab shall perish . . . And the dogs shall eat Jezebel . . . and none shall bury her . . ." (2 Kings 9:7, 8, 10). Jezebel was attacked and destroyed by the dogs of her own powerful aggressiveness.

One can presume that, upon hearing the news, Jezebel might have turned toward God, seeking His forgiveness, and have been spared, as Nineveh was spared when the inhabitants turned from their evil. But not Jezebel. Second Kings 9:30 says, when she heard the news of her impending disaster, ". . . she painted her eyes, and adorned her head, and looked out of the window." She became the painted woman for which we remember her today. Focused on her beauty and her pride to the end, she looked outward instead of into her own heart, where she might finally have seen her evil and been healed. The Bible tells us though our sins are as scarlet, God can wash us white again, as white as fresh snow or lamb's wool. There was still time for Jezebel to become the chaste one God had created her to be, even then.

The story ends strangely. Two or three eunuchs threw Jezebel from the window to the street below, where horses trampled her to death. There was a great banquet of celebration because the wicked witch was dead, and when they came back to bury her body, only her skull, her feet, and the palms of her hands were left. The dogs came and ate her up. So the beautiful, brilliant, charismatic Queen Jezebel, the most powerful woman in the land, who played the harlot against God, was overcome by two or three chaste men, immune to her seductive power, who acted as agents of God's justice. Nothing remained but the palms of those hands she had used to destroy a king, a nation, and herself.

How ugly the wicked witch really is, especially when she is confronted by the Light of God.

> Confronted by the Light,
> What once seemed bright
> Recedes, ashamed, into the darkness.
> And what lay in shadows
> Is transfigured by the sun.
> My life
> Become as though a twilight
> And a dawn.
> No longer are old boundaries drawn
> For building caskets for the living,
> Gone are the walls;
> The veil is rent asunder
> And I stand alone
> In nakedness
> Before the Throne
> Stripped of illusions and delusions,
> Motives and desires exposed,
> Only a skeleton of who I am remains
> Bleached in white flames.

Oh, that this tomb
Might be the womb
From which I can emerge
To greet my destiny.
This coffin be the cradle
Into which the Spirit breath might blow
On these dry bones
Scattered upon the desert of my soul,
Making me whole,
A heart of flesh created from this heart of stone.

12

Beyond the Power Plays

What do we do when we come face to face with the Jezebel within us? Our souls cry out, as Paul's did when he saw his inner shadow, "... I do not do what I want, but I do the very thing I hate.... I can will what is right, but I cannot do it. For I do not do the good I want, but the evil I do not want is what I do ... Wretched man that I am! Who will deliver me from this body of death?" And the answer Paul discovers? "Thanks be to God through Jesus Christ our Lord!" (Romans 7:15, 18, 19, 24, 25).

God is able to deliver us from the wicked witch. But first, we must be willing to acknowledge she belongs to us. With all her potential evil and destructiveness, we must be willing to take the responsibility for her actions, and this is never easy. We don't like having to admit things like this to ourselves. We would much rather try to excuse our unkind or manipulative behavior, blaming our moods on someone else. How many times, when I have yelled at Lucian or the children or have been rude to a friend, have I complained, "I'm under a lot of pressure right now," or, "I guess it's just the wrong time of the month for me," or, "Someone has upset me," instead of getting to the root of the problem and confessing, "I acted terribly toward you. Would you please forgive me?" We won't have any success overcoming the wicked witch if we try to weasel out of her bad manners.

It won't do any good to try to camouflage her, either. Putting a veneer of insincere sweetness over her works about as well as putting perfume on Miss Piggy, who in spite of her long white gloves and satin dress, is still a pig. Our wicked witch won't go away simply because we have tried to disguise her. In fact, those parts of ourselves we try hardest to hide are often the most obvious. The wicked witch, which the Bible calls our sin nature, can't be changed by human effort alone. She is not only an emotional problem; she is also a spiritual problem, and she requires a spiritual transformation.

We also must be willing to admit our powerlessness about the whole situation, which means getting to the point of recognizing, "I really messed up, Lord, and if You left it up to me completely, I would probably mess up again." It is always a blow to our egos to have to admit something like that. It goes against the grain of the element in us that insists upon our walking on the grass when we see a sign asking us not to; we do it simply because someone said we couldn't. Ultimately we must hand our inner Jezebel over to God, who is the only one more powerful than she is, anyway. He died for her so we could be freed from her power over us, so we may use our proper power for His glory and honor and praise.

Like Jezebel, however, our witch will fight to the death. We'll not have an easy time handing her over. One of the problems will be that we have grown accustomed to her. Even though we're ashamed of the things she does, we have gotten used to having her around. Perhaps we've even developed a strange fondness for her, as we might for an old acquaintance with whom we've been through a lot of experiences. So we treat our witch much as my son Jonathan did a dead squirrel we found in our yard one day. She had been a very mild-mannered squirrel, and we had grown fond of watching her scurry around. When we took her out into the garden to bury her, Jonathan could not bear to think about never seeing her again, so he buried her body, but not her tail, which he lovingly draped over a rock, as a memorial. Somehow, it didn't get the job done. We explained to Jonathan it was going to be necessary to bury the whole squirrel. We, too, must be forceful about burying our wicked witch, as forceful as the eunuchs with Jezebel when they threw her from the window and into the hands of the Living God.

A grain of wheat must fall into the ground and die before it can be transformed into new life, and our wicked witch must be handed over to death so the good in her can be released. Within our negative, selfish, and egocentric natures lies the seed of great creativity and life, which when brought into the light of God's presence, can be transformed into some of our greatest strengths. As in the story of *The Wizard of Oz,* inside the cold tin man lies the potential for a heart; inside the cowardly lion is a place for courage; and within the empty head of the straw man is the potential for a brain. Underneath the rags of every wicked witch lie the garments of a queen.

Once we recognize our sin nature, admit it belongs to us, agree with God about its ugliness, recognize our powerlessness to reform it with our own effort, and hand it over to God, then He will take care of the rest. It doesn't matter if our problem is jealousy or gossip; envy or adultery; greed or overeating; a quick temper or possessiveness; a lust for power, as Jezebel had; or all of them put together. God transforms all these ugly attributes into pure gold. In fact, I have found the process He uses in my life, as He deals with my wicked witch, very much like the process used to refine gold.

First the gold must be dug carefully out of the ground by someone like God, who is skilled at recognizing its value. God knows all that glitters in my life isn't gold, but He also sees deep into the crevices of my heart, and sometimes He finds a nugget that no one else would find. He then takes it and pounds it until He separates the clay from the ore. He removes all the distractions and desires of life that cling to the gold, clouding its brilliancy and tarnishing its luster. He washes it, removing all the dirt particles with the water of His Holy Spirit, until He has prepared the gold for the crucible.

In the intense heat of the refining fire, the inner impurities of the gold, which lie too deep to be seen, are burned away. In the crucible God brings up to my consciousness those hidden thoughts, broken dreams, and deep wounds that drain me of vitality. When I am in the crucible, I see those parts of myself for which Christ died on the cross. Masks cannot last. They burn up very quickly. Illusions of myself disappear. In the fire of God, I am stripped down to the bare bones of the essence of my metal. "The crucible is for silver, and the furnace is for gold. But the Lord tests hearts" (*see* Proverbs 17:3). In the white heat of God's love, He tests my metal, making it strong and preparing it for service.

Peter tells us, ". . . Now for a little while, if necessary you have been distressed by the various trials that the proof of your faith, being more precious than gold which is perishable, even though tested by fire, may be found to result in praise and glory and honor at the revelation of Jesus Christ" (1 Peter 1:6, 7).

Sometimes it feels very lonely in the crucible of the refiner's fire, and these are often the times when God seems very far away from us and we feel abandoned in a dark night of our soul. But the master craftsman always stands beside his fire, watching intently, deeply concerned about the final outcome of the ore he tests, adjusting the flame so that the metal will not be consumed by more heat than it can bear. "And He will sit as a smelter and purifier of silver, and He will purify the sons of Levi and refine them like gold and silver, so that they may present to the Lord offerings in righteousness" (Malachi 3:3 NAS).

In addition to purifying the gold, the refining fire also makes it soft and workable, ready to be hammered and shaped into one of the treasured vessels fashioned by the craftsman for use in the Temple, vessels in which right offerings may be presented to the Lord, upon the altar of His service. The final destination of the transformed wicked witch is the Temple of the Lord. But to get there, we must be willing to submit our power to His power.

Gail once had a wonderful dream about this process. She dreamed she was brought into a temple and given a beautiful gold crown to wear. She had been made a queen. She was then brought into the presence of God. Her first impulse was to bow down before Him in adoration, but she hesitated because she feared that if she did she might lose her crown.

God has given every woman in the world queen potential, and He longs for us to use it to the glory of mankind as the helpers and the mothers of the living. But to be queens, we must be willing to bow before the King in adoration and submit our power for His use.

The root of the word *crucible* is the same as for the word *crucifix*. The Bible calls this refining process being crucified with Christ. It is dying to ourselves that we may live in Christ. This death is at the heart of what it means to abide in Christ so that He may abide in us and we may become gradually transformed into His likeness. Because of this Jesus told His disciples they would be able to do the very work He had done, and even greater work, for He would be living in them and empowering them with His power. Paul referred to this process when he said, "For it is God who is at work in you, both to will and to work for His good pleasure" (Philippians 2:13 NAS). When Christ lives within us, not only does He enable us to live a life pleasing to Him, but He also causes us to desire to live that life.

To come through the crucible is to have been crucified with Christ and to be resurrected with Him, transformed into new creatures empowered to love with His love. This happens when we bring our gifts and talents into the service of the King of Love.

I suppose God could transform us in an instant, but it doesn't happen very often. The process of being made whole usually takes a long time—indeed it takes a lifetime—and like learning anything new, there are a lot of failures at first. *What if the wicked witch returns?* we ask in panic. She will. All we must do is simply repeat the process, putting her back in God's hands. *Won't He get tired of forgiving me?* we wonder. *Especially so many times in one day?* Of course not. It is His delight to make us whole. "For if while we were enemies we were reconciled to God by the death of his Son, much more, now that we are reconciled, shall we be saved by his life" (Romans 5:10). "Who shall separate us from . . . the love of God in Christ Jesus . . ." (Romans 8:35, 39). "If God is for us, who is against us?" (Romans 8:31).

I remember the day I realized this principle as a mother. Once more I felt I had failed miserably, and I was so discouraged. Then I remembered God's complete sufficiency, and I wrote in my journal:

It's the reckoning that counts after all. Thank You, Lord, for reminding me of that today. I have been feeling so at a loss—knowing I needed to be a better mother, but not knowing how, wondering if You weren't going to have to perform some cataclysmic event in my life to make me new. And then I remembered the reckoning—that act of the will that refuses to listen to words of discouragement and inadequacy, but reckons all those mistakes I've confessed to You as being dead with Christ and alive with Him in newness of life. I've done my part—I've asked You to take my mothering and make it into what You want it to be. And now I will believe that You have done Your part, too, and have already made me new. When my mistakes come between me and Your best plan for my life, help me to remember to confess and then to reckon they are dead, so I can start again to walk with confidence within the power of Your love.

However, we must take a final step in this process of dealing with the wicked witch. We must be willing to welcome her back into our lives again, once she has been transformed. Like the father in the story of the prodigal, who watched and waited for the return of his son, running to meet him with great joy and thanksgiving, so must we watch and wait for the return of our prodigal selves. Often we are like the older brother in that story and fear embracing our wicked witch once more, becoming pious and moralizing toward her when we see her returning from her journey in the far country of God's crucible. We say, "You can't trust her, you know." Unable to believe God could have transformed her into a beautiful queen with a crown of gold, we won't receive her back. But the older brother in each of us needs to embrace the prodigal who also is in us, for when this happens, a deep inner healing can occur, which can only be described as part of the mystery of God's grace.

A lovely woman I will call Jean once told me of such an experience in her life. As a teenager she fell in love, became pregnant, and underwent an illegal abortion. Although she never told anyone of this, over the years, the knowledge of it darkened her spirit. In spite of all the people who loved her and her many valuable attributes, and although she knew God had forgiven her, she had never been able to forgive herself for what happened.

Jean has a special way with teenagers, perhaps because of her experience, and as her children were growing up she enjoyed an open, casual relationship with many of their friends, who frequently confided in her. She was home alone one morning when she heard the doorbell ring, and as she opened the door her daughter's best friend fell, weeping, into her arms. During the hour that followed, the girl, spilled out a story of great inner pain and struggle. The preceding day she had undergone an abortion.

"You know, Barbara," Jean said to me, with tears glistening in her eyes. "As I embraced that frightened and unhappy teenager, holding her to me and stroking her hair, I realized I was also embracing another needy teenage girl, from long ago, who needed my love and understanding, too. For the first time I was able to forgive myself for a mistake I had carried in my heart for twenty years."

There are beautiful results when we embrace the wicked witch God has transformed. Forgiving ourselves brings His healing love into the deepest wounds within our hearts, making us whole once more.

13

That Gentle and Quiet Spirit

Once a woman learns how to handle her wicked witch, she is ready to learn how to plug into the right kind of power—a power that enables her to be all God has created her to be. She can find the source of that creative femininity and use it in the midst of going to work, taking the dog to the veterinarian, or selling drinks at the school carnival. For most of us life seems to be a perpetual spilling of ourselves, a draining away into tiny streams going in all directions, until we feel depleted and barren, caught up in a whirlwind of activity that pulls us into fragmented pieces of the women we long to be. It doesn't have to be that way. Peter, the tempestuous disciple, gives us an answer. "Let not yours be the outward adorning with braiding of hair, decoration of gold, and wearing of fine clothing, but let it be the hidden person of the heart with the imperishable jewel of a gentle and quiet spirit, which in God's sight is very precious" (1 Peter 3:3, 4).

What is Peter saying to today's woman? He tells us that in the hurriedness of our lives, it doesn't matter if we are dressed in the finest designer clothes, have just been to the beauty parlor, or have the most elegant jewelry to wear; unless we can go through our days with hearts that are gentle toward others and spirits at peace, we will not be the precious jewels God has made us to be. Peter directs us to look inward, into the silent recesses of our hearts, to see if we can't discover those hidden wellsprings of our femininity and our spirituality.

Since the earliest times the most universal symbol of womanhood has been the earth—Mother Earth—into which seeds of life are sown and in which growth occurs slowly and persistently in secret and in silence. The way a baby grows within a mother, protected in dark stillness, pictures the feminine spirit. For a woman to find that spirit, nurture it, and grow from it requires times of quiet. In the stillness a woman becomes receptive and open to new direction in her life, and when she is quiet, she is also most open to God. By going to the still places of her heart, she is renewed, replenished, and invigorated by God's Spirit to become the helper to mankind and the mother to the living for which she has been made.

Anne Morrow Lindbergh reminds us:

If one sets aside time for a business appointment, a trip to the hairdresser, a social engagement, or a shopping expedition, that time is accepted as inviolable. But if one says: I cannot come because that is my hour to be alone, one is considered rude, egotistical or strange. What a commentary on our civilization, when being alone is considered suspect; when one has to apologize for it, make excuses, hide the fact that one practices it—like a secret vice!

Actually these are among the most important times in one's life—when one is alone. Certain springs are tapped only when we are alone. The artist knows he must be alone to create; the writer, to work out his thoughts; the musician, to compose; the saint, to pray. But women need solitude in order to find again the true essence of themselves: that firm strand which will be the indispensable center of a whole web of human relationships.

Women seem to know this intuitively. I remember the terribly stressful time in my life surrounding Jonathan's arrival. Lucian and I were about to move to the community where he would at last begin his medical practice. Nervousness and excitement followed us through the final weeks of his residency, as he intensely studied for his medical boards. I spent my time packing boxes, cleaning the house to be sold, and lining up the carpenters and painters needed to repair the house we were about to occupy. In the midst of the turmoil the social worker from the adoption agency called with the exciting news we had waited so long to hear. Our first child was coming—the very next day! We had twenty-four hours to prepare a nursery, and I was frantic. It's strange to hear you are imminently to become a mother, when you didn't even know you were pregnant. I simply refused to put my firstborn in an empty packing box from the discount store. So I began running around in circles, as Lucian said, much like a mother hen, about to lay her eggs, who has discovered her nest is strewn all over the yard. Our neighbors and friends pitched in heroically; shortly the guest room had been transformed, as though by some magic wand, into a beautiful nursery. There was one task remaining however: the job of transforming me.

Late in the night, after Lucian went back to the hospital and all the friends had gone, I sat in the blue and white rocking chair in the dark nursery. At last I found my way to that path that leads to my inner springs, and there I wept my tears of joy and gratitude, pouring out my fears and anxieties before the Lord. In that quiet place He walked beside me through all the emotions most women have nine months to feel, preparing me to be a mother. By the next afternoon I was ready to give Jonathan something much more valuable than a freshly painted crib and a bottle of warm milk. I had been energized to give him a mother with a gentle and quiet spirit in the midst of all the frenzy going on around us. If only I could remember this now, each and every day.

From going inward a woman finds the resources she needs to give on the outside. Only when we have gotten things right in our hearts can we truly share. For it is from the center of our spirits God pours through us, if we will let Him. A man gets on his horse and charges out, in action, to right the world's wrongs. A woman goes to her inner hearth and tends her fires as she waits to find the way and the courage to do what is necessary. "I will lead you into solitude and there shall speak to your heart" (*see* Hosea 2:14). It is a feminine way of dealing with life.

Of course we often forget to do this. We react and act from those reactions, halfway down the road before we remember to look inside. The Bible gives a wonderful illustration of the wise and the foolish way to handle our circumstances in the story of two sisters, Mary and Martha.

It had not been a very good day for Martha, what with all she had done to get the house ready for Jesus and those disciples He always brought with Him. She and Mary had been working since before dawn, airing out the bedding, sweeping the courtyard, and arranging the flowers before they started preparing the food. Martha wished Jesus wouldn't always come on such short notice. The fruit at the market had not been as good as it should have been, and Martha had a terrible time finding a large enough cut of meat. It had taken her half the morning to get everything she needed. Mary kept telling her Jesus would much prefer it if they kept things simple so they could enjoy His visit, but Martha had a particular way she always liked to do things. People had come to expect a certain standard when they came to Martha's house, and she was proud of that. She had been ashamed of herself for scolding the servants in her haste and had even burned her hand getting that second batch of almond cakes from the oven. Perhaps those had not really been necessary, but they were, after all, her specialty. Her friends from Jerusalem always complimented her when she served them. Now that Jesus had come, it was time to put all the food on the table. *Where was that Mary?* Martha wondered. Didn't she know Martha couldn't do all the work by herself?

As she stepped out of the kitchen to look into the courtyard she saw Mary sitting right next to Jesus, listening to him intently. True, Mary had done everything Martha had requested that day. The two sisters had worked equally hard to get things prepared. But as soon as Jesus came, Mary had disappeared, to be with Him.

"Lord," Martha called bitterly from the kitchen doorway. "Do you not care that my sister has left me to serve alone? Tell her then to help me!"

Jesus replied, "Martha, Martha, you are anxious and troubled about many things; one thing is needful. Mary has chosen the good portion, which shall not be taken away from her." (*See* Luke 10.)

Mary sat beside Jesus, listening to His teachings. She would worry about overly elaborate preparations another day, when Jesus was gone. She had done her work in advance. But Martha was distracted by too much serving when a simple meal would have sufficed and she, too, could have sat listening to Jesus.

It isn't easy for modern women to take the time to sit at the feet of

Jesus. The world constantly intrudes into our lives, bombarding us with stimuli. How far away we are from the women of primitive times, who not only didn't have our distractions, but also had a built-in time of introspection once a month. During a woman's menses she was considered taboo and was isolated from the rest of the tribe. This meant that for a four- or five-day period, on a regular basis, she didn't have to clean, cook, or nurse the children. It must have been wonderful. It was an opportunity for her to get back in touch with herself, a time when she could reevaluate her relationships, her role in those relationships, and her priorities. No doubt if she used her time wisely, she returned to her family renewed and refreshed, with a new perspective on those complications that perplex our lives. She returned ready to begin again.

Many of us do not take that kind of time today, and we have consequently lost our way to our inner wells. We have lost the source of the power that would enable us to live meaningful and abundant lives, have lost touch with God, and have also lost touch with our own uniqueness as individuals. As Sylvia said to me once, "You know, I'm always identified as somebody's mother, somebody's wife, or by the work I do. If all these things were suddenly taken away from me and someone were to ask me who I am, I wouldn't have any idea how to answer them."

Refinding our way to the source of our gentle and quiet spirits takes some very active planning, and those of us raised to believe we should always put ourselves last will find this an especially difficult task. But we must know ourselves to be able to act from those selves. We can't pour from nonexistent or broken jars and by making the time we need for ourselves, we can mend our water jars from which God would have us pour His love upon a thirsty world. Christ would mold us into sturdy vessels, replacing our deadness with vitality and our feelings of uselessness with purpose, energizing us and putting us back into working order so we can go about the business for which He has created us, whatever our jobs happen to be.

For me that time is often when everyone has gone to bed. My inner biological clock doesn't cooperate very well with an early morning quiet time. Although my body gets up and starts moving at 7:00 A.M., to pack lunch boxes and put up Rebecca's ponytails, my soul and my spirit rarely catch up until after 10:00. So my time is at night. Sometimes I save a chore to do until then, because I like to putter around in my nest, when the rest of the family is asleep. Often, I read my Bible. And I talk to the Lord. I try to listen to Him. I also talk to myself, and I try to listen to myself, spending time with myself in the presence of God. Sometimes I quietly stand over the members of my family and pray for them before I turn back the covers on my side of the bed.

But these times of quiet are not always enough. Every now and then I take the telephone off the hook and spend an entire morning in silence. Once a year I even pack the children off to day camp, stock the freezer, and let the family fend for themselves while I spend a week at the beach, with the girls. It's a marvelous way to get back in touch with my femininity. The four of us sleep together in one room, dormitory style, giggle a lot, and eat M & Ms for supper without worrying about setting a bad example for the children. We enjoy an opportunity to talk casually and unhurriedly about our lives and problems, asking advice from one another. But we also give each other plenty of time to be alone, to walk on the beach and feel the sand between our toes; dancing in the sunlight with the waves again, as we did when we were girls; shedding our responsibilities along with our beach robes, to find ourselves again. We learn to know our names once more, and we fill our jars from which we will pour all through the fall, winter, and spring to come. Some might think this trip is selfish, but it is more than just a good time. It is also a responsibility we have to those who are closest to us and who need from us what only we can give. We can give best from a gentle and quiet spirit we have taken time to nourish with a week at the beach with the girls. Seek peace, the Psalmist tells us, and actively pursue it.

Often when we think of peace, we think of immobility. But God's peace makes us alive. Everything about God is alive, for He is Life; so to find His peace is not to be freed from activity or even from conflict: It is to have soundness and wholeness in the midst of whatever is going on in our lives. To have a gentle and quiet spirit is not necessarily to be tranquil, but it *is* to be able to function with a measure of contentment, for the Source of Life itself replenishes us.

> Peace is the centre of the atom, the core
> Of quiet within the storm. It is not
> A cessation, a nothingness; more
> The lightening in reverse is what
> Reveals the light. It is the law that binds
> The atom's structure, ordering the dance
> Of proton and electron, and that finds
> Within the midst of flame and wind, the glance
> In the still eye of the vast hurricane.
> Peace is not placidity; peace is
> The power to endure the megatron of pain
> With joy, the silent thunder of release,
> The ordering of Love. Peace is the atom's start,
> The primal image: God within the heart.
>
> MADELEINE L'ENGLE
> *The Weather of the Heart*

I saw this peace on Lib's face one day as I turned the corner at the grocery store with my cart and watched her scanning the soup section. She looked wonderful. She had just celebrated her seventieth birthday and said she had never been happier in her life. "There is a new peace and serenity at this juncture in my life I never dreamed possible. I know myself better than I ever have, have finally come to terms with my limitations, and have quit struggling to be what I'm not. I have also realized the great value of relationships. How very wealthy I feel today!" A softness enveloped Lib, a warmth, and an openness to be met. I found myself wanting to embrace her, drawing some of her warmth into myself. She radiated joy. Not *happiness:* She radiated *joy.* We spoke of her brilliant husband, John. "You know," she said, "it hasn't been easy living all these years with a genius. We haven't had any really serious problems, but it has taken me a long time not to feel inadequate about myself because I couldn't measure up to John. Now I can see all I have contributed over the years as well and how important I have been, too, and all I wish for now is just more time to live. It's so wonderful being alive!" Lib reminded me of an ancient Chinese story of a Rainmaker.

It seems that in a remote village a long drought had parched the fields; the crops were endangered, and the people faced starvation and death in the months that lay ahead. The villagers did all they could. They prayed to their ancestors; the priests took the images from the temple and marched them around the fields; but no ritual and no prayer brought the rain. Finally in despair they sent for the Rainmaker. When at last the old man arrived, they rushed to him, telling him they would give him anything if only he could make it rain. He told them all he needed was a quiet place where he could be alone to spend his time doing all the things one ordinarily does each day. They gave him a small hut in which he lived, and on the third day it rained.

The Rainmaker is an illustration of those rare people around whom life blossoms as they simply go about their ordinary business—not ostensibly helping others, loudly praying, or devising mammoth programs—yet around them things seem to happen. People breathe freer, children laugh, and everyone feels accepted just the way they are, experiencing that kind of love which heals like a gentle rain restoring life to a parched field.

For all in whom Christ has been born there is a tiny seed of Rainmaker potential called the Holy Spirit. It can grow and flower into the kind of quiet heart that makes life happen and cocreates with God. He beckons all of us to come sit beside Him, leaving for a while the demands that fill our days, so we may listen to His voice and rekindle the Rainmaker heart lying within us. "If any one thirst, let him come to me and drink. He who believes in me, as the scripture has said, 'Out of his heart shall flow rivers of living water'" (John 7:37, 38).

Are we willing to take the time to turn inward to allow God to teach us the secrets for a woman's ear, believing He has called each one of us in this hour to bring rain to a sterile world? I hope so.

God sometimes calls us to be solitary souls

To walk as pilgrims on the narrowed path
Not always wide enough to share,
Enduring separation there,
Away from laughing friends
Who touch and sing,
Who warm and bring
Companionship along the way
Into the quiet of His heart
Into the desert of His love.

God sometimes calls us to be set apart

And when He calls
We often shrink from following His Will
Into the way that seems so barren
And so still
So waterless
So cold and bare
It seems no other voice
Has ever echoed there.

Yet from those desert skies,
Upon the unimpeded plains,
In God's own place
Fall all the elemental forces
Of His Grace.
It's in the desert
That the water and the wind,
The earth and fire,
Can merge within the soul
Upon the sacrificial pyre
Of solitude
One offers in the deserts of God's Love.

God sometimes calls us to be solitary souls.

14

What *About* Submission?

A story is told of Queen Victoria that one day she and Prince Albert argued, and he locked himself into his room. The equally angry queen knocked loudly on his door, demanding to be admitted.

"Who is there?" Prince Albert asked.

"The queen of England," came a haughty reply. The door remained closed.

She knocked again, he asked the same question, and she gave the same answer. The door remained closed.

Then there came a gentle knock.

"Who is there?" Albert asked once more.

"Your wife, Albert," was the queen's reply. And Prince Albert opened the door to his room.

Only after the wicked witch has been tamed and we are stripped of all our illusions about her are we able to take a good look at the inner dynamics operating in our close relationships. After we have acknowledged our secret wishes to be the most powerful and have found the source of our gentle and quiet spirits, we can finally take an honest look at what Peter means when he says, "Likewise you wives, be submissive to your husbands, so that some, though they do not obey the word, may be won without a word by the behavior of their wives, when they see your reverent and chaste behavior" (1 Peter 3:1, 2), or what Paul is saying when we read, "Be subject to one another out of reverence for Christ. Wives, be subject to your husbands, as to the Lord. For the husband is the head of the wife as Christ is the head of the church, his body, and is himself its Savior. As the church is subject to Christ, so let wives also be subject in everything to their husbands. Husbands, love your wives, as Christ loved the church and gave himself up for her" (Ephesians 5:21–25).

The issue of submission remains a volatile subject for women, and people express a variety of opinions about these biblical references. I have heard Christian speakers teach that women are to be completely obedient to their husbands in all things at all times, submitting to every wish and command, never questioning their judgment, but trusting God to change their minds if they are not in His will. On the other hand others teach that a woman can be released from submission if her husband asks her to break one of God's commandments. She submits first to what she believes God wills in her life and only secondarily to her husband's desires. Others have argued that submission forms God's chain of command and that, although the husband is the head of the household, the wife is the heart. Others have said a mutual submission should exist between the sexes, that marriage is a partnership, and each partner should love in such a way that they are able to work out mutually acceptable solutions. Some teach that the concept of submission is no longer relevant for our times. They argue that Paul gave a guideline applicable to the culture of the early Church, but that new guidelines must be discovered for ways in which the male and female can relate today. Consequently this entire issue of submission is one area in which I feel not all the votes are in yet. I try to stay in the middle of the road, which is not always a safe place to be, because you can get shot at by both sides.

I suppose that after talking with scores of women on this subject over the years and hearing many of their stories, the issue seems a lot more complicated to me than I had at first thought. I've listened to women subjected to emotional and even physical abuse punishable by the law, yet they endured it in the name of submission. I've met women who are not permitted to choose their own clothes, also under the guise of submission. But I've also talked to women so strongly opposed to the concept that they fought their husbands tooth and nail over the smallest issue, determined not to be submissive. I've met women who believed all the responsibilities in the home should be so equally divided between a husband and a wife that they wouldn't even put their husbands' socks into the washing machine along with their own clothes.

Carol told me perhaps the most graphic tale about the misuse of the principle of submission I have ever heard. Her husband came from a very conservative religious background. He took very seriously his authority and responsibility as the head of the household; that was why he said he managed their finances so carefully. Carol had to ask permission to buy even a pair of shoes. He also felt he had a responsibility to know where she was at all times and frequently called her from work four and five times a day to check on her. Once when he discovered she had gone somewhere he had not wanted her to go, he took away her car keys for several days. She soon began to resent these intrusions into her privacy, but she felt guilty about her resentment because she was trying to be a submissive wife. Carol found herself lying to her husband about her whereabouts and about how she spent her money. When he caught her lying, he berated her severely. This went on for several years and got a lot worse. After lengthy counseling and much prayer, she finally left him and moved into an apartment with a friend. Their marriage had been destroyed on the very principle that should have made it more workable. Obviously this was not what Paul had in mind when he wrote that husbands should love their wives and wives should submit to their husbands.

Indeed, focusing on the principle of submission to the exclusion of many other verses in the Bible about relationships does seem to pit the sexes against each other in an unhealthy way. I remember the first time I ever heard a lecture on this subject. I had been a Christian about two years. How I had missed hearing about submission up to that point is beyond me, but I had. I was also still a bride, and Lucian and I had just come through a difficult first year of marriage. The auditorium was filled with almost a thousand young people, most of whom were single, as we listened to one of the foremost conservative authorities on the Christian home. His first lecture was about wives submitting to their husbands. All the men grinned broadly the entire hour, and I noticed the women squirmed a lot. I kept receiving knowing looks from my husband, which said, "I hope you're listening to this!" At the conclusion there was a loud burst of applause, and the men cheered wildly as we women politely clapped our hands and glanced at one another rather guiltily. But the second lecture was about the importance of husbands loving their wives. The tables had turned. Suddenly the women were relaxed and had become quite animated. The men began to stare at the floor. Now I nudged Lucian. At the close there were no cheers and whistles from the men, but we women clapped just as hard as we could. I had the strange feeling we were on two different sides, two separate teams warring against each other, and I didn't like the way it felt at all.

I believe God created men and women to be collaborators, instead of competitors, as we all work together to make this world a better place. To both sexes God gave the command to subdue the earth, and that tall order requires the cooperation of everyone. God created us to use our separate gifts so we blend in unity, completing each other instead of competing with each other.

But God also gave the man and the woman different functions in life. Our gifts are different. The male functions as the primary initiator. He instinctively leads, rules, and protects when he is around a woman, whereas the woman quite naturally responds to his lead, follows, and adapts when she is around a man. This doesn't mean a woman cannot lead or that a man cannot respond; it only means this is the primary way in which the sexes instinctually relate to each other. It is not a comment on who is the most capable or the strongest or the best, merely an observation of the way in which each sex uses its strengths.

A man has physical power and the power to reason, which he can use either to lead or to dominate the female. He can protect her or overpower her. These masculine traits need to be restrained by love in order to be used properly. On the other hand a woman has a greater emotional power and sexual power, which she can use either to illuminate or manipulate the male; she can enliven him or seduce him into getting her own way. Her power needs to be restrained by submission in order to be used properly. That husbands should love their wives and wives should submit to their husbands is an observation of how each submits to the other in love. The male and female must both submit, but they submit to each other in a different way.

Genesis 29 beautifully illustrates this concept with the story of Jacob and Rachel meeting at the well. A large flock of sheep had gathered there and were thirsty. They needed to drink the water from a well that was covered by a very heavy stone. Rachel stood beside the well, carrying a jar she could use to draw the water from the well, but she was not strong enough to lift the stone. Jacob was strong enough to remove the stone, but he lacked a water jar with which to draw the water. Each one needed the other to function in an important capacity, and when they worked together, the flock was watered.

This interaction is similar to the description of the first marriage. The Bible says Adam and Eve became one flesh. Eve was bone of Adam's bone, created to be his counterpart in order to complete him. The two of them were created for mutual interdependence in which the woman took her life from the man but gave it back to him again. God meant for all who are married to be one flesh also. Our sexuality, even in today's world, is in a deep sense a drive toward that oneness and wholeness that are God's plan for the sexes. It is still in marriage that the greatest potential of "knowing" another human being is possible. As men and women merge intellectually, spiritually, emotionally, and physically they expand their knowledge about each other and of themselves. For this reason God declared it was not good for the man to be alone.

God intended the mutual interdependency between the man and the woman to be cemented by love, for without love they could not truly be one. But marriage was not meant to be a mutually exclusive symbiotic attachment of two halves, but the honest meeting of two complete people, two individuals neither of whom dominated the other. The love we should share is the kind of love in which we both want to see the other person grow and mature, whether or not it brings us any advantage. This love takes pleasure in watching the other freely live. It is not possessive or overbearing; Paul describes it in 1 Corinthians 13:4–8, when he says, "Love is patient and kind; love is not jealous or boastful; it is not arrogant or rude. Love does not insist on its own way; it is not irritable or resentful; it does not rejoice at wrong, but rejoices in the right. Love bears all things, believes all things, hopes all things, endures all things. Love never ends. . . ."

What a different picture from the vicious circle that can develop when the sexes compete. When a woman tries to dominate a man, she weakens him and causes him to become irresponsible. This makes him begin to feel powerless. The more powerless he feels, the more likely he is to try to overpower the woman; the more overpowered the woman begins to feel, the more power she seeks, in order to protect herself. Love is lost in the battle. Ideally a man must love his wife with a love that neither dominates her to use her for his own selfish purposes nor tries to possess her as his toy. And the woman must relinquish her desire to manipulate the man or to mother him in a way that ties him to her possessively. Both should love each other with a love that releases even as it submits. Sometimes they will work together; sometimes they must work apart. Sometimes one partner will lead, and sometimes the other must lead. There will be moments when each finds he must work alone.

In a world where women are ready to take more responsibility and men would like more time for nurturing the children or for pursuing their own creative interests, each couple will have to come up with their own unique arrangement. In this period of transition in the roles between the sexes, it is not always easy. Often the man finds it as difficult as the woman does. A man who grew up in a home with a mother who fulfilled a traditional role may suddenly discover that his job transfer forces him to cope with his wife's career as well as his own. When he comes home from the office, he may be left with the responsibility of getting dinner and putting the children to bed, so his wife can attend a class. In addition he may be longing to satisfy some of his own needs for a more varied life. He may want more time off to pursue his interests. Finding himself caught in the conflict of being the successful career man his mother always told him women wanted and being the kind of partner today's woman desires, he also discovers himself sharing more of the responsibilities at home as well. An effective system of mutual self-expression within an intimate relationship such as a marriage takes a lot of flexibility and open-mindedness from men as well as women these days.

Lucian and I have worked on this very problem while I have been writing. He cannot always easily give me the time, support, and space I need to create. After all, in the beginning Lucian contracted for the traditional model of marriage. True, he had seen me doing things like write in college, and he was more than happy for me to teach school during his medical training, so we could pay his tuition and buy groceries. We shared many responsibilities back then. He took on an extra job in addition to his schoolwork and helped me clean our apartment on Saturdays. But in the back of his mind he always thought when he got out into practice, I would stay home and do some volunteer work in my spare time. I did that, but after nine years I began to feel restless and unfulfilled. While he had been busy in his training, I had learned how to do a great many things by myself, to the point where, since he was seldom able to help hang curtains or take care of the house, I had asked for an electric drill one Christmas. I felt that uneasy feeling you get when you know you're not doing what God has created you to do. I knew I was not using most of the gifts He had given me.

When the opportunity came for me to lecture, Lucian and I made a joint commitment to my ministry, just as we had jointly decided upon every other major area in our marriage. But it hasn't always been easy for either one of us that I have such a time consuming job. Invariably Lucian is on call at the hospital when I am supposed to be out of town speaking. Twice he has left a patient in an examining room, to pick up a sick child at school, while I was away. Once our cocker spaniel even had to spend the day at the office, because she had run away while I was out of town. Recently I left for two weeks to work on my book, and Lucian packed lunches and put up ponytails in addition to his responsibilities at work. Fortunately some great friends pitched in with the car pools and invited the family for dinner. I also received some marvelous help from our teenage baby-sitter, Lisa. But there have been some rough spots. Lucian sometimes gets tired of adapting to my schedule, and I tire of adapting to his. We eat out more often, and I'm not having lunch with my friends the way I used to, either. Slowly, however, we're beginning to find a balance that works for us, and Lucian now has the benefit of living with a more satisfied woman again.

Of course I've given up my aspirations for winning the mother-of-the-year award as well. I'm not making it to as many of the children's activities as I used to, and once or twice I missed making it home on time to meet the school bus. But Jonathan and Rebecca are learning to take more responsibility and to make sacrifices that have not hurt them at all. They are developing a lot of confidence in themselves and are learning some good self-discipline. They've also used this time to know their dad better. Since I cannot always monitor their arguments, they are learning how to work out their own differences as well. As Lucian and I learn to move into a relationship of mutual collaboration, of giving each other the freedom to grow and expand into all God has created both of us to be, I hope we also give our children an example of the kind of love God meant men and women to have for each other.

In spite of all the give-and-take, inevitably in any marriage, however, there comes a moment when someone must be responsible. From the beginning God has held the man ultimately responsible for the welfare of his family. The Bible says in 1 Corinthians 11:3 that Christ is head of every man and man is the head of a woman. This headship is a responsibility that every woman should honor.

I like the way Lane Adams has described the man's headship when he says:

> As I see it, there is no way for a husband to demand submission on the part of his wife without violating the command of God for him to be loving. Let the love of Christ in him have that constraining effect on a wife and he may discover that she is no longer rebellious or fearful about the idea of submitting to that kind of leadership in the home. . . . There is no suggestion that a woman submits to a man's leadership because he is superior or she is inferior. As I see it, the only possible reason she should submit to his leadership is because of the awful responsibilities he has in the eyes of God. When we elect a government official to a position of responsibility, we must confer on him the necessary authority to fulfill the responsibility. The same thing is true in the home. It is only because of the responsibility that the man must have the authority. However, since he cannot compel the woman to give him that authority, the only way he will ever get it is for her to confer that authority on him. The reason she should confer that authority on him is that he bears the responsibility that God has laid on his shoulders.

Ultimately submission should be the life-style of every Christian, for we must all be willing to submit our power, our lives, and our love not only to God for His use and for His service, but also to others. True submission requires a great deal of maturity, however, for it comes only from a heart that looks past self-centered needs and desires, to the needs of another. Submission is an attitude of interdependency and a sense of community that spring only from a strong individual who bends his will around the will of another for the sake of love.

At the heart of learning how to love is our willingness to be fluid in our relationships with others. In an intimate relationship to which we have made an earnest commitment and in which we willingly experience the pain of coming back time and again to work out our differences, we may learn more about ourselves and about love. Because of this, marriage is such a marvelous vehicle for stretching and expanding our understanding of life.

Within Lucian's wedding band is inscribed "One in Christ," and learning more about what that means has been the major goal of our marriage. But that phrase also applies to any close relationship. We are all to be one even in our diversity, never clinging to each other possessively or dominating each other so thoroughly that we stifle individuality, but thrusting each other out to newer heights of becoming. Ideally we become a giant tapestry in which we are all woven together in such a way as to enhance our individual colors and textures as we cooperatively form a background, with our relationships, for the larger work of expressing God's love in our world.

Weave

Weave, weave, weave us together
Weave us together in unity and love.
Weave, weave, weave us together.
Weave us together, together in love.

We are many textures, we are many colors,
Each one different from the other.
But we are entwined with one another
In one great tapestry.

Weave, weave, weave us together
Weave us together in unity and love.

We are different instruments playing our own melodies
Each one tuning to a different key.
But we are all playing in harmony
In one great symphony.

Weave, weave, weave us together
Weave us together in unity and love.

A moment ago, still we did not know
Our unity, only diversity
Now the Christ in me greets the Christ in thee
In one great family.

Weave, weave, weave us together
Weave us together in unity and love.
Weave, weave, weave us together.
Weave us together, together in love.

ROSEMARY CROW

15

The Power of a Woman's Love

A rare, black lily grows in our garden. In the early spring it pushes through the earth as straight, directed, and purposeful as any masculine symbol could be. But after it emerges, is warmed by the sun and softened by the rain, it begins to unfold into the most delicate stalks and leaves, reaching high into the air. This lovely and very feminine unfolding could never take place, however, without the force and the focus necessary to break the plant through the ground. It portrays something of the interrelatedness between men and women. Mankind has developed over the last several centuries through the thrusting aggressiveness of the masculine attributes, but without an equal development of the feminine, our culture will not unfold properly. If we continue to deprive ourselves of the usefulness and uniqueness of all that is feminine and continue to value only the masculine traits, we will produce a firm, resolute, and purposeful world, but one that will never flower.

For this reason I believe it is now critical for women to strive courageously to unearth once more the wellsprings of what it means to be a woman. We must clear away the debris of neglect, ignorance, and misunderstanding surrounding the feminine way of going about life. We must remove our own feelings of self-doubt and low self-esteem, which inhibit the flow of our own best selves. When we have overcome these barriers, we will allow our femininity to pour once more upon the parched ground of our present world. If we will do so, I believe we can enable the world to flower again.

In primitive cultures men and women are forced to collaborate with each other in order to survive. Each depends upon the other functioning as hunter, crop tender, water carrier, and food gatherer, in order to live. Although, in most societies today, the sexes no longer lean upon each other so obviously for basic physical necessities, we still rely on each other for our emotional and spiritual survival. The man still needs the woman's warmth and vision, and the woman still needs his reason and discernment to temper her emotion and her intuitive wisdom.

The sexes continue to relate to each other much like opposing poles in an electrical field, igniting each other and creating a vitality that each can not find alone. This is as it should be, and although we are currently experiencing tension between these opposing poles, perhaps these signs of growth will mature into a new way of relating that can enhance us all.

New growth never appears without conflict and change. Jesus reminded us that a grain of wheat must fall into the earth and die before it can produce a harvest. Perhaps we would do well to try to keep in perspective the discontent and doubts, the strivings and the longings that seem part of the struggle between the sexes, for perhaps they are merely birth pangs. Naturally these pains distress us and a great deal of social suffering is accompanying them. We are experiencing upheaval in the process, and for the moment we perceive a greater separation between the sexes than has ever before existed as we try to differentiate ourselves from each other. Clearly we see excesses and destructiveness. But perhaps this separation will in time lead to a unity more balanced, creative, and mature than the sexes have ever before experienced. When we begin to relate to each other more as individual human beings and less according to stereotyped roles, will we not all experience richer lives?

Growth and change in the relationship between the sexes is natural and should not surprise us. Everything that has life changes. Certainly we would do well to watch carefully the direction of this growth, pruning it of all that is harmful for either sex and directing its shape, but we should not try to stunt it. We must allow it to blossom, and we can do this when we trust in the creative process that rules the rest of the universe, also trusting the Creator Himself, who has made us male and female. Although we presently find ourselves in a winter season between the sexes, there is much cause for hope, because that which occurs beneath the surface feeds the buds that in due time will emerge in the spring.

Artists often hold the position of visionaries in a culture and frequently herald change and growth. Since the turn of this century, the poets and authors, the painters and the composers, have all reflected in their art the disintegration of an old order. Many have also reached out to try to grasp a vision of a new world. Although some say we now live in the final century of history and that we are seeing a vision of the New Jerusalem, no one can know for sure. The Bible says that even the Christ does not know when the end will come and that we must try to live our lives day by day, working to discover how, in the future, we can live creatively together.

The Bible tells us that new wine must be stored in new wineskins, and within the Bible itself we can discover the container in which to house a new way of relating between the sexes. Now as never before, we can reach toward the potential of experiencing that spirit of cooperation and community that is very close to the vision of *koinonia* Paul gave to the early church. He outlined a fellowship based on partnership, created from a spirit of generous sharing, exactly the opposite of that grasping spirit so characteristic of our times. All too often we look out for ourselves, selfishly manipulating one another to make sure our own needs are met. Because of these actions and attitudes, we neglect to meet the needs of others. In the New Testament Paul spoke of a relationship consisting of a mutual sharing of property, of services, of gifts, and ultimately of Christ Himself, which becomes a celebration of life and of love as each person strives to discover how he can best meet the needs of another. As in the story of the loaves and the fishes that Jesus multiplied to feed the hungry group of people who came to hear Him teach, when we experience that kind of fellowship with one another, miraculously everyone feels satisfied. We enjoy the essence of the sacrament of Christian communion, the sharing of God with us, God in us, and God through us.

But how do we learn this technique? Ann Morrow Lindbergh, in her classic book about women, *Gift from the Sea,* offers these words:

Fear destroys the winged life! It can only be exorcised by its opposite, love. When the heart is flooded with love there is no room in it for fear, for doubt, for hesitation. When each partner loves so completely that he has forgotten to ask himself whether or not he is loved in return; when he only knows that he loves and is moving to its music, then, and then only, are two people able to dance perfectly in the tune to the same rhythm.

Her image of a dance draws me because it relates so beautifully to what the Bible teaches about life. A ballet celebrates life in all its aspects, and life is an expression and a revelation of God. The name for God, *Jehovah,* comes from the same root as the word for "life." When God breathed His Spirit into mankind, He gave each of us part of that life. Therefore to celebrate life is to celebrate God, and to be in touch with life in one another is to know more about God. Jesus declared He had come into the world in order that we might have life and have it more abundantly, pressed down, shaken together, and running over.

When men and women collaborate as one, through the power of the living Christ, using their gifts cooperatively for the whole of mankind, they function in the same way the Godhead itself functions—in unity—and they truly experience life. This portrays a great mystery, for although the Trinity consists of three distinct personalities, each with a separate function, at the same time they remain one. And although the sexes are distinct and different, each with separate gifts, we may also relate as one. Then we move together in such a fashion that we learn what it means to love and to be loved in return. For God is also love. Love is the expression of His life and of His creativity, and ultimately through love's real power celebration of life becomes possible. Only as we learn to love one another can we begin to become cocreators with God, for love fills us and empowers us to become what we have been created to be.

What does this mean specifically for a woman? Life seems to flow through a woman from that place where she was created in God's image, much as the sap flows through a tree. This life, inextricably bound to her sexuality and her creativity, forms the essence of her femininity. It reasserts itself in her life in cycles, rising and falling throughout the months and seasons of her years, each season having its own special beauty. The energy, tied to her feminine expression, weaves itself mysteriously in and out of her existence. A woman's power comes from this source, which is at the heart of what enables her to be a helper of mankind and a mother to the living. Each of us must choose how to use this life force, this spirit God has breathed into us, for ultimately, a woman discovers her highest value in loving. Although she must learn to recognize this powerful force and experience it within herself, it is best expressed in relationship.

How we decide to use our power today will vitally affect the outcome of our world. We can nurture, or we can starve. We can bring life, or we can withhold it. We can help, or we can seek our own personal power. Our major task as women is to learn how to allow the sap of life to flow within the boundaries of love, unselfishly using our power to create instead of to destroy, to encourage instead of to dominate, to bring new growth and new life instead of to stifle. We can learn to do so only by surrendering our power to God's power, submitting our egocentric desires and personal power plays to the One who enables us to serve mankind.

A woman who experiences her own power and submits it to God sees the rainbow of her femininity and finds herself transformed through the discovery of her own value. Then no room remains for a poor self-image or for counterfeit role playing. She learns to love herself and to see her worth because she discovers the reason for which God created her.

Perhaps Jesus implied the necessity for this kind of love when He spoke to the Samaritan woman that day as He sat at the edge of Jacob's well. Tired from a long journey, He asked her to lower her jar and give Him a drink of water. It was at the heat of the day. That hour was an unusual one in which to draw water. But Jesus acted in an even more unusual fashion, when He spoke to the woman at all; for she was a Samaritan, and a great hostility existed between the Samaritans and the Jews. She also wore the mark of a married woman, and it was improper for a strange man to speak with her. So rather than give Him the water He requested, she did a very characteristically feminine thing: She began to ask Jesus some questions. Slowly He began to reveal His divine identity to her, revealing her identity as well, unveiling her as an adulteress, stripping her of all her false illusions of herself in order that He might make her whole.

"If you only knew who I was," He had said, "you would be asking Me to give water to you, and if you asked, I would give you running water. It would so fill you that you would never again thirst, for it would become in you as a spring, bubbling continually within you forever."

It must have sounded good to her. She carried a heavy water jug, which felt especially cumbersome because she was compelled to carry it in the heat of the day, in order to avoid the glares and taunts that must have come her way from the other villagers. "Sir," she replied, "give me this water so that I won't have to constantly come all this way each day, carrying my jar alone." But Jesus also saw the burden she carried in her heart. He knew the stone that needed lifting before she could receive His gift. So He gently but firmly pointed to the problem. "Go call your husband," He said.

The woman answered, "I have no husband," and Jesus honored her honest revelation of herself. He always does. "You're right," He said. "The fact is, you have had five husbands, and the one you are living with now you are not married to." It was only then He told her who He was, the Christ, who had come to pour His love on such as she.

And how did the Samaritan woman respond? The Bible tells us she left her water jar beside that well and hurried into the village. I suppose Jesus had to get His own drink of water after all. But at that moment she became so filled with the living water of His love that she began telling all she saw, "Come quickly. The Messiah has come. The Christ is in our midst!" Jesus lingered in that village several days, and many more believed in Him because of what the woman had first told them, for Jesus had transformed her adulterous love into the kind of love that flows as running water, touching all around her with creativity.

Every woman who uses the power of her love selfishly, to achieve only her own desires, is like that woman at the well. Our love is unchaste and adulterous. And like the Samaritan woman, we might try to hide this egocentric love, coming to the well when no one else is looking, in the heat of the day. But we can never hide our motives from God. He will firmly but gently unmask our flaws, if we will let Him, not that He might stand in punitive judgment over us, but in order that He might remove our hearts of stone and fill us with His love.

When we are willing to look honestly at ourselves and allow the Christ to fill us with His living water, God releases in us the kind of love that brings healing and vitality to all around us. Our lives become as a watered garden, able to satisfy the desires of our own hearts and to quench the thirst in the souls of others.

As a woman allows herself to express the positive power of her love she animates all she touches, and she carries with her a spark of the divine. For when she functions from her true essence, she brings truth, creativity, joy, and ultimately God Himself into the lives of those she meets. This then becomes her life work in the midst of whatever she may be doing, for her qualities as helper, as counselor, as comforter, as encourager may be expressed, no matter what her life circumstances happen to be and no matter what they might have been before.

God created each one of us from His love in order that we might experience love and then serve that love. Sometimes it means willing submission. Sometimes loving requires us to resist. Sometimes it means going to tell, and sometimes it means knowing when to remain still. But we will discover that as we open ourselves in deeper and deeper ways to God's living water we will become more filled with that love, which is the expression of His life, and we will experience on a more profound level what it is to be loved and what it is to have life. When we seek to learn more about the ways of love, a veil begins to be removed from our eyes, and we begin to be transformed into the image of God.

In 2 Corinthians 3:16–18 (NIV) Paul says:

> But whenever anyone turns to the Lord, the veil is taken away. Now the Lord is the Spirit, and where the Spirit of the Lord is, there is freedom. And we, who with unveiled faces all reflect the Lord's glory, are being transformed into his likeness with ever-increasing glory, which comes from the Lord, who is the Spirit.

Although he may not have realized it, Eugene O'Neill wrote a play about this dynamic of which Paul speaks, when he created *The Great God Brown.* In his play all the characters are veiled, for they all wear masks. The main character, Sibyl, who like the Samaritan woman, is a harlot, also wears a mask. But during the course of the play, she begins to wear her mask less and less, revealing herself as she really is to all the other characters. As a result, they, too, begin to remove their masks, revealing the best within themselves.

From the beginning of time, women have tended the sources of creative energy. We have stoked the hearth fires, drawn the water, have borne and nourished the children, and have converted primary energy to make it available for life. Women carry beauty and inspiration, and those who draw near us should draw closer to this life-changing energy as well.

If we would turn mankind once more toward this creativity, which is from God, it will take all the emotional and spiritual maturity each one of us can develop, and it will require the removal of our masks. For we will be able to accomplish this task only with unveiled faces, through the power of our love. We must continue to recognize the embryonic in all its forms, nourishing it, pruning it, watering it, fertilizing it, giving it the air and the space within which it can develop according to its own inner laws of growth—whether this growth is in ourselves, in a child, or is new potential in a spouse or in a friend. We must never try to own or to possess, but merely to hold it for a while, until all that is new is ready to be born. Then we must release that life, thrusting it out to bear fruit of its own. This should be our joy as well as our responsibility as women, for in this way we give ourselves to our own femininity, to mankind, and to our God, reflecting His glory and becoming the glory of mankind.

My prayer for today's women is that we will turn our palms and unmasked faces upward once again, receptive to the generative power of God, so that we might use our feminine power to become vessels of strength and agents of love.

Bibliography

Bibliography

Barclay, William. *New Testament Words*. Philadelphia, Pa.: Westminster Press, 1976.

Campbell, Ross. *How to Really Love Your Child*. Wheaton, Ill.: Victor Books, 1981.

Carroll, Lewis. *Through the Looking Glass*. New York: St. Martin's Press, 1977.

Claremont De Castillejo, Irene. *Knowing Women: A Feminine Psychology*. New York: C. G. Jung, 1973.

Clark, Stephen. *Man and Woman in Christ*. Ann Arbor, Mich.: Servant, 1980.

Conway, Jim. *Men in Mid-Life Crisis*. Aurora, Ill.: Caroline House, 1981.

Dobson, James. *What Wives Wish Their Husbands Knew About Women*. Wheaton, Ill.: Tyndale House, 1975.

Dowling, Colette. *The Cinderella Complex*. New York: Summit Books, 1981.

Elliot, Elisabeth. *Let Me Be a Woman*. Wheaton, Ill.: Tyndale House, 1976.

Friedan, Betty. *The Second Stage*. New York: Summit Books, 1981.

Graham, Billy. *The Holy Spirit*. Waco, Tex.: Word Books, 1978.

Guggenbuhl-Craig, Adolf. *Marriage—Dead or Alive?* Dallas, Tex.: Spring Pubns., 1981.

Gundry, Patricia. *Woman Be Free*. Grand Rapids, Mich.: Zondervan, 1979.

Harding, Esther. *The Way of All Women*. New York: Harper Colophon, 1970.

Ibsen, Henrick. *A Doll's House*. Chicago, Ill.: Coach House, 1979.

Jewett, Paul. *The Ordination of Women*. Grand Rapids, Mich.: Eerdmans, 1980.

_____. *Man as Male and Female.* Grand Rapids, Mich.: Eerdmans, 1975.

Johnson, Robert A. *She: Understanding Feminine Psychology.* New York: Harper & Row, 1977.

_____. *He: Understanding Masculine Psychology.* New York: Harper & Row, 1977.

Kelsey, Morton. *Caring: How Can We Love One Another?* Ramsey, N.J.: Paulist Press, 1981.

L'Engle, Madeleine. *Walking On Water.* Wheaton, Ill.: Harold Shaw, Pubs., 1980.

Lewis, C. S. *The Four Loves.* New York: Harcourt Brace Jovanovich, 1960.

_____. *Till We Have Faces.* New York: Harcourt Brace Jovanovich, 1957.

Lindbergh, Anne Morrow. *Gift From the Sea.* New York: Pantheon, 1955.

_____. *War Within and Without.* New York: Harcourt Brace Jovanovich, 1980.

Luke, Helen. *Woman: Earth and Spirit.* New York: Crossroad Pub., 1981.

Marshall, Catherine. *The Helper.* Lincoln, Va.: Chosen Books, 1978.

Marty, Martin. *Friendship.* Allen, Tex.: Argus Comm., 1980.

May, Rollo. *Love and Will.* New York: Norton, 1969.

Mead, Margaret. *Male and Female.* New York: Morrow, 1977.

Miller, Jean Baker. *Toward a New Psychology of Women.* Boston, Mass.: Beacon Press, 1977.

Miller, Keith. *Please Love Me.* Waco, Tex.: Word Books, 1977.

Morgan, Marabel. *The Total Woman.* Old Tappan, N.J.: Fleming H. Revell, 1973.

Rogers, Dale Evans, and Carlson, Carole C., *Woman.* Old Tappan, N.J.: Fleming H. Revell, 1980.

Sanford, John A. *The Kingdom Within.* Ramsey, N.J.: Paulist Press, 1980.

_____. *The Man Who Wrestled With God.* Ramsey, N.J.: Paulist Press, 1981.

Scarf, Maggie. *Unfinished Business: Pressure Points in the Lives of Women.* New York: Doubleday, 1980.

Stedman, Elaine. *A Woman's Worth.* Waco, Tex.: Word Books, 1976.

Stedman, Ray C. *Body Life.* Ventura, Calif.: Regal, 1979.

Stone, Nathan. *Names of God.* Evanston, Ill.: Moody Press, 1944.

Tournier, Paul. *The Gift of Feeling.* Translated by Edwin Hudson. Atlanta, Ga.: John Knox, 1981.

————. *The Strong and the Weak.* Translated by Edwin Hudson. Philadelphia, Pa.: Westminster Press, 1977.

————. *To Understand Each Other.* Translated by John Gilmour. Atlanta, Ga.: John Knox, 1967.

————. *The Whole Person in a Broken World.* New York: Harper & Row, 1981.

Ulanov, Ann. *The Feminine in Jungian Psychology and Christian Theology.* Evanston, Ill.: Northwestern University Press, 1971.

Van Scoyoc, Nancy J. *Women, Change and the Church.* Nashville, Tenn.: Abingdon, 1980.

Waltke, Bruce. "1 Corinthians 11:2–16: An Interpretation." *Bibliotheca Sacra* 135: 46–57.